THE PUPPETEERS

THE PUPPETEERS

Studies of Obsessive Control

GERALD ALPER

NEW YORK
FROMM INTERNATIONAL
PUBLISHING CORPORATION

Published in 1994 by Fromm International Publishing Corporation
560 Lexington Avenue, New York, New York 10022

Designed by C. Linda Dingler

Manufactured in the United States of America
Printed on acid-free recycled paper

First U.S. Edition 1994

Library of Congress Cataloging-in-Publication Data

Alper, Gerald.
    The puppeteers : studies of obsessive control / Gerald Alper.– 1st U.S. ed.
        p.   cm
    Includes bibliographical references.
    ISBN 0-88064-160-6 (cloth : alk. paper) : $19.95
    1. Manipulative behavior. 2. Manipulative behavior–Case studies. 3. Control (Psychology) 4. Cults–Psychological aspects. 5. Single people–Psychology–Case studies.   I. Title
BF632.5A47   1994
153.8'52–dc20   94-33056
                                                                                    CIP

5 4 3 2 1

To Tom, Steve, and Anita

TABLE OF CONTENTS

PREFACE

The Puppeteers is about the loss of freedom—freedom that is lost through being dangerously unaware of the extent to which one is being controlled, and freedom that is lost through too complacently believing (which is perhaps far more common) that by controlling something, someone, or oneself, one has thereby enhanced one's personal power.

The three studies that follow exemplify, each in its own way, this theme: that of obsessive control and seduction, the devious ways by which people fall prey to external, and often internally imposed, manipulation. They are based on actual patients I have known and worked with, and are presented as they were originally seen by me through the prism of psychoanalytic psychotherapy. Accordingly, the focus is always on the solitary person and the singular perspective. Although the names and certain circumstantial details have been changed in order not to betray the confidentiality to which they are entitled, the events are portrayed, and especially, the psychological dynamics are delineated, as accurately as I can make them.

The first study is that of a disciple (Matthew) of a counter-culture cult, one of the pockets of desperate utopian hope that periodically spring up in America, who manages to extricate himself without deprogramming or reprogramming, by naturally and traumatically "bottoming out" when the cult catastrophically collapses. Although historically the birth and death of the cult that is chronicled in this necessarily long first section preceded by many years, and was already completely written prior to, the David Koresh/Waco, Texas debacle, which continues to preempt a perhaps disproportionate share of the national consciousness, the uncanny foreshadowing of the processes of cult indoctrination and ultimately group insanity cannot help triggering a shock of recognition in the contemporary reader.

The second study depicts a man (Paul) caught up in a telemarketing sweatshop, a "boiler room": a place without frills, without illusion, and without any pretence (because there is no need for it) of corporate dressing up of what is sometimes complacently acknowledged as healthy, all-American, me-too greed.

The third is a portrait of a gathering of lonely hearts, the "singles scene," and of a woman (Emily) caught in the tender trap of obsessive love.

While all three were restored to a sense of themselves sufficient for them to go on and lead more or less autonomous lives, unlike other psychotherapists who write about their work, I do not dwell on the details of their recovery, and as the reader will see, this is not a technical book about treatment methods.

I depart from the prevailing trend in the technical literature of anatomizing and analyzing the people I write about. I try to steer clear of the kind of characterological distortions that are an unavoidable side effect of the continuing upsurge in this country of biological psychiatry, in which individuals who appear as subjects in clinical studies currently being published in no way seem identifiable as human beings. Indeed, more often than not, in these studies there does not seem to have been even an attempt to portray them as individuals; what is portrayed, rather, are discrete, segmented behaviors meant to embody and presumably to verify preconceived clinical hypotheses.

Since my aim—in opposition to this trend—is to give a picture of both the person and his world, I use an impressionistic style intended to convey at least some of the texture of lived experience. My psychotherapeutic interventions (and I certainly had my fair share of those in the course of the therapy upon which these studies are based) are, as the reader will note, kept to a bare minimum. Accordingly, each of the three studies is divided into two distinct but interrelated parts: an initial long, narrative, naturalistic picture, as faithful as I can render it, of what I believe is the essence of what has been conveyed to me through the conduit of therapeutic engagement, and a subsequent extended commentary in which I present my reflections on what I think I have learned from the experience I have been privy to. A final comment on my style: although it is often narrative, I never play omniscient author. Thus, for example, thoughts and feelings attributed to Tony Thunder, the founder of the cult, who so far as I know never once in his life set foot in the office of a psychotherapist, are those that were witnessed, experienced, or inferred by Matthew and then reported to me. In this regard, the rendering of Tony Thunder, as cult "father figure" to my patient, Matthew—while admittedly extensive—is in principle no different from standard depictions of transferential parental surrogates who traditionally are meaningfully described without ever having been directly seen.

Although there are great differences among lives in a cult, in a "boiler room," and in the singles scene, I choose to stress the similarities. I believe the ubiquitousness of my unifying theme, in every cross section of American life, justifies this strategy. To paraphrase Hannah Arendt, who spoke of the banality of evil, there is a contemporary banality of obsessive control, of human exploitation of the self by self and others, that is as readily glossed over. Instead, what seems to capture the attention of not only the public but the mental health profession are clear-cut cases of unmitigated and at times even monstrous abuse perpetrated upon a proliferating catalogue of victims: children of alcoholics, children of incestuous parents, children of narcissists, children of dysfunctional families, and so on.

By contrast—and in spite of the periodic eruption of bizarre cult behavior like that chronicled in the long opening section—*The Puppeteers* is not a book primarily about people who live outside conventional experience, or who are driven by aberrant inner needs to break society's rules. Rather it is about what happens to people who live by the rules, or who enforce the rules—but do so obsessively, inhumanly, and mechanistically. Matthew, who abandons himself to what he thought was the higher form of life embodied in a cult; Paul, who passionately wanted to climb the corporate ladder of success, no matter how many times he fell off; and Emily, who nearly lost her mind in her search for love— each personally symbolizes, in one degree or another, a type of human exploitation prevalent in our time that I have termed "behavioral puppetry." After the narrative portion of each study, I compare and make explicit the common elements of seduction, manipulation, and obsessive control that are woven into each of the particular worlds. In the last chapter of the book, from a phenomenological standpoint I attempt to gather together some formal properties of behavioral puppetry that I believe run through nearly every stratum of American society.

Throughout, I am mindful of the writings of the great British psychoanalyst W. R. Bion, who wrote profoundly and with precision of the near-impossibility of faithfully recreating perishable moments of elusive clinical truth.

Rather than explicate or analyze, it is better to show. And that is what I have tried to do.

PART I

AMERICA THE BEAUTIFUL

TONY THUNDER

"He asked me if I thought I might be able to fly and—I know this sounds weird—I wasn't entirely sure I couldn't."

By "fly," I knew that Matthew meant with his arms and his legs, with his body and his head, propelled solely by some inner paranormal gravity-defying psychic force. He wasn't psychotic. If I had to pin a diagnostic label on him, I might have settled on a neurotic identity crisis, triggered by an adjustment panic that had followed the traumatic collapse of a cult he had been symbiotically enmeshed in for the past three years, which, if it had been a fair assessment (i.e., that he was normal and not psychotic), was that much more confounding because it left to be explained just how an intact, highly intelligent mind could be so toyed with.

And that is what Matthew, increasingly bitter since he had returned six months previously from California in a state of panic, had resolved: that he had been toyed with. It was the dominant theme he never tired of harping upon, what he most wanted me to understand so as then to be able to explain it to him, as, leaning forward in his chair, his voice often breaking down into bursts of hysterical, self-deprecating laughter, especially when he came to the Götterdämmerung in California part, he passionately retold and relived his introduction to, indoctrination in, and odyssey through a strange cult.

It became clear to me, and this was borne out the first few months I knew him, that before Matthew could begin to speak about himself it would be necessary to exorcise the toxic residue, as he had experienced it, and the invasive presence of the charismatic leader of the cult; and this could only be done by a cathartic recreating of the peculiar spell Tony Patrano managed to cast on anyone who drew close to him. I understood that Matthew needed me vicariously to sense Patrano's aura, to see him as Matthew saw him so as better to analyze him; and this meant that my first patient was going to be a proxy: Tony Patrano. It was a task made simple by the fact that Tony Patrano was a natural and incorrigible storyteller, and there was no story he more loved to tell than the story of his own life, or really his destiny, as he came to see it.

Tony's adoptive parents did not want him to be Jewish (and because of it, later neither did he), but he was. He was not sorry he could not remember his biological parents, who were both dead by the time he was three, which relegated him to a foster home; neither could he remember being rescued by the Sicilian woman who came to claim him, and—especially after her husband died shortly thereafter—seemed driven to raise her newly gotten son to be the best that he could be.

If there were things he did not remember or did not want to remember, there were also things he was stubbornly not told: not until he was ten was he informed, at the insistence of the child welfare worker, of the fact that he had a schizophrenic biological older sister, Jean, who for years had been institutionalized at Creedmoor Psychiatric Center; and not until he was fifteen did he piece together a multitude of clues and gather the courage to face down his indomitable mother, who grudgingly admitted that yes, he was an adopted son.

The revelation could not have come at a darker time, precipitating as it did his first adolescent crisis, and what in retrospect he would consider one of the turning points in his life. The crisis consisted of his bitter and heartbroken conclusion that he was thoroughly disliked by his peers, and that he probably never would be liked. It was a conclusion that baffled him in its unfairness, but seemed forced upon him for many reasons: tall, gaunt, and oddly solemn, he could find almost nothing in common with his classmates—he loathed sports, considered schoolwork a trivial exercise at best, and dreamed only of making his mark, astonishing people by some unsuspected and undreamed-of accomplishment. What it would be, he didn't know, and this—added to his growing alarm that he was becoming a pariah, (exacerbated by the disclosure of his adoption)—made him despair of ever finding the means of dramatically imposing himself upon the minds of his contemporaries in the only way that would be meaningful to him, the way he had been fantasizing about for years.

That was his crisis. The turning point arrived with his startling conviction, which he would subsequently refer to as his "epiphany", his angry determination, and his zealous vow to himself to take his life into his own hands and virtually to create—though willpower—the destiny for which he believed he had been chosen. And Tony Patrano prided himself on his iron willpower, and remembered being riveted by the sight of his first hero, Vincent van Gogh, as depicted in the movie *Lust for Life*, holding his hand in a candle flame to prove his mettle until the flesh stank. It was the kind of glorious fanaticism that could successfully defy even the greatest odds. It was the kind of fanaticism that his sister Jean—whom he now visited three or four times a year and who each time, as he was about to depart from the hospital grounds where they would stroll arm in arm, would clutch at his shoulder and whisper, "I love you, Tony"—tragically lacked. Although the more often he visited his sister the more he pitied her and the closer he felt to her, he was aware how much he hated the idea that there could be anything so binding as a genetic linkage between two minds that he viewed, literally and symbolically, as mirror opposites.

He would set to work, then, although only fifteen, to strengthen even further an already powerful will so as to prepare for the task that he was certain lay ahead. It meant spending even less time on his schoolwork and more time in the confines of his room as he struggled grimly to take total control of his life; and in such a state of perplexed self-involvement, it was merely a question of time before Tony encountered the magical-sounding dictates of positive thinking. He became an instant convert, first to

Napoleon Hill's classic *Think, and Grow Rich*, and then systematically working his way through the standard works of mind control, from scientology to neurolinguistic programming to autosuggestion, to video cassette motivational tapes to be heard subliminally, while sleeping. Tony experimented with them all. As soon as he hit upon an idea that made sense to him, that promised to offer a better shortcut to mastering his destiny (as he now chose to think of his future), which he increasingly craved, he would put it into practice: first on himself, and then on the nearest available classmate. To his delight—it was the first positive thing that had happened to him in years—Tony discovered that he was very good at this, and while his classmates still decidedly did not like him, they now took notice. Something about his lean, conservatively dressed, six-foot frame was almost dashing, and the mysteriously serene self-confidence with which he expressed whatever he currently professed to believe in, despite his tone of superiority, was nevertheless impressive. Indeed, an uncanny self-confidence—the ability to speak calmly, logically, and positively, regardless of how fantastically removed from the realm of common sense his ideas might seem—would become the adult Tony Patrano's signature style.

And gratified, and emboldened by the impact his emerging persona was having upon his classmates, Tony resolved to push even further and break new ground in his quest for total mind control. He would now stand before his bedroom mirror, sometimes for hours at a stretch, in an attempt to master the technique of self-hypnosis, based on the positive-thinking belief that in order to be fully in command of one's life, it was necessary to take charge of the last great frontier, the Unconscious Mind. But it was a technique he could never learn; no matter how hard he tried, it continued to elude and frustrate him, until one afternoon, standing before his mirror, he suddenly realized why—and he stopped trying. It was a realization that Tony would come to count as a second turning point, and it consisted of this: that since his willpower was so strong, his unconscious mind, the life force that secretly drove him, must be that much more powerful, and *that* meant that no one, not even himself, could ever hypnotize him, because his mind was *unconquerable*.

It was a turning point even more exhilarating than the first because it pointed in a direction that until now he had never seen, and Tony now understood that part of the course his life would surely take would be to utilize his extraordinary force of personality to mold and teach less fortunate minds. He was only sixteen years old, but he recognized that it was time to pass along some of the incredible things he had discovered, in less than a year, about how to control the human mind. It led to writing his first book; sequestering himself in his room, sometimes staying up the entire night, sometimes roaring with laughter at the imagined delight of his readers (alarming his mother, who would pound on his locked door). Tony wrote steadily and furiously for seven straight weeks, and did not stop until he had a completed manuscript in hand.

He called it *Meet Your Secret Powerful Self,* and it was his wildly enthusiastic, boyish version of the classic Horatio Alger rags-to-riches story combined with Charles Atlas's boy-who-got-sand-kicked-in-his-face story, recast as a do-it-yourself manual and rallying cry to the world's teenage weaklings to transform themselves—via the magic of Tony Patrano's original positive-thinking tips—into towers of inner strength. It put him in touch with an electrifying sense of his imaginative power and what years later he would simply allude to as "my creative genius."

Thrilled with this first accomplishment, Tony journeyed from his home in Mount Vernon to Manhattan, for the very first time, to hand deliver the treasured manuscript to Lucille Tinling, a publisher of mystical, self-improvement, and feminist works, whose name he had found among the advertisements of a scientology paperback. And his heart raced when she seemed graciously to accept the submission of the young author, and sweetly told him to return in a month's time.

It was with the boundless idealistic hope of the creative neophyte that Tony returned to reap his reward—and instead collected his manuscript.

Sympathizing with his undisguised chagrin, Lucille Tinling sighed, then, cocking a quizzical eye, inquired, "Did anyone—you know, your mother, for example—read this?"

"No," said Tony, who wondered what that had to do with anything.

It was his first taste of a presumable expert utterly failing to grasp the splendid scope of his intentions; and like analogous disappointments that would eventually follow, it not only did not discourage him, it made him more determined than ever to prevail. Of such rebuffs, Tony liked to say, with prideful stoicism, "It was only the opening shot of a war."

When he was seventeen years old he managed to graduate from high school (despite the fact he had done literally no homework at all for two years), and with the money he had saved from summer employment, he took a share in a tiny apartment in Manhattan in order to begin his new life. It was natural that he would gravitate to the wide-open field of high-pressure sales, and that he would accept for his initial full-time job the grandiose challenge of selling something no one wanted, industrial chemicals, to someone no one wanted to talk to, an industrial chemicals purchasing agent.

In the future, it would be designated as one of the "great stories" in the unfolding narrative drama of his life, as it was lived and chronicled in the mind of Tony: how, in a job infinitely beneath his talents, a milieu he would characterize as "low-life carnival scum," he would nevertheless rise to the stature of a star performer, which he accomplished primarily by virtue of his inexhaustible commitment to devising whatever strategy it took to produce a sale. Whereas fellow salesmen were content to fall back upon such outdated scams as "the widow" (i.e., calling up under the pretence of making a benefit sale to help out a fictional widow whose husband was supposed to have been tragically killed while driving a nearby truckload of industrial chemicals), Tony would be experimenting with more sophisticated neurolinguistic sales pitches, meant to implant subliminally the necessary cues in the buyer's unconscious mind. Sometimes they worked, and sometimes they didn't. But what always amazed his envious co-workers was his refusal to become even slightly depressed at the failure of a sales pitch (an almost automatic, universal reaction among high-pressure salesmen), and because of his relentless, and to them inhuman, smile following the loss of a sale, no matter how big or important, they dubbed him "the Joker," after the Batman character.

Tony let none of it bother him. By now he could handle someone not liking him, especially someone he did not respect, and he took his revenge in his growing pleasurable conviction that whenever he put his mind to something, he could beat anyone who cared to compete with him. At the end of his first full year of employment, at the age of eighteen, he had earned fifty-five thousand dollars, which, given the year (1967), was a great deal of money by any standard. It enabled him to move into his own apartment, near Gramercy Park, to dress in style and to advance in earnest upon yet another frontier: women.

Seeing no reason to change what had proven so successful, he decided to use his favorite tools—knowledge of how to control the unconscious mind of the other, awareness of where the telling weaknesses lay and what the corresponding leverages should be—in his pursuit of women. He was not ashamed that his technique of flat-out manipulation was tantamount to cold-blooded seduction, he was proud of it; and he approached the seduction of a woman with the same tenacity that he approached the seduction of an industrial purchasing agent. Since it meant so much to him, it was not surprising that Tony, who spent most of his evenings roving from one "hot" singles club to another, would in time become an accomplished seducer of women, both young and old; and given his penchant for continually embellishing his mythic sense of himself, it was also not surprising that tales of his fabulous seductive powers would be added to his repertory.

His favorite concerned Maureen, a seventeen-year-old from Ireland, who worked illegally as a maid in a sleazy midtown hotel: she had been instantly swept off her feet by Tony and was prepared to do anything for him, sexually, except surrender her virginity. And merely because she was so genuinely, noncoquettishly adamant in her refusal, and not from any special interest in her, Tony resolved he must have her. Years later, when telling the story, he would pound his thigh in anticipation of his listener's dismay at hearing the diabolical details of his seduction. How, over a two-week period, mainly through tireless poker-faced repetition, he managed to persuade Maureen that there were two orifices to her vagina: a central one containing her hymen, and in which intercourse takes place, and a very minor, secondary one, which was located just below the real opening, and had nothing to do with intercourse or becoming pregnant. Tony explained that often men and women who liked each other but were not yet ready to have intercourse would use this secondary orifice as a means of experiencing safe pleasure, and when she seemed sufficiently convinced, he gently inserted his penis into the place where it allegedly mattered least.

Some time later, while walking in the street with Maureen, Tony announced he had a confession to make. "What?" she asked, and bracing himself, he replied, "We've been screwing for the past two weeks!" At this punch line, Tony would always rock with triumphant laughter, and then conclude, "She threw a fit at first. But I calmed her down, and eventually she accepted it."

By the time he was twenty, he was a solid success in business, measured against the accomplishments of his peers, most of whom were college students, and an even greater success with women, measured against his personal yardstick of proven seductive charm and recorded conquests. In spite of this, however, he was far from satisfied: not unhappy, as he had been prior to his first major turning point as an adolescent, but, as he would now put it, philosophically discontented. At twenty, he fancied himself an amateur, yet important young philosopher: someone who could put his finger on the core of a problem, who could slice through a maze of distractions and get to the bottom of whatever was wrong.

And what was wrong, according to the young philosopher, was that something was missing: not from himself, as he had mistakenly believed as a tortured adolescent, but from society. He could not say what the missing piece was; he only had a nagging sense of a certain heartlessness, indecisiveness, and lack of vital meaning that he found everywhere. It would be selfish and mean-spirited, Tony reasoned, to simply hedonistically reap the rewards of his own energy, which certainly would be substantial, while the rest of America languished in a state of painful aimlessness. In order to clarify what he should do, he decided to read the great books and study the great minds. Although he had disdained entering college, feeling that no one else could educate him as well as he himself could, a dialogue on an equal footing with great thinkers was another matter. Applying the same tenacity of will to this as to everything else he did, Tony began regularly to take out up to a dozen books from several libraries each week.

He did not feel obligated to read every one of them or even a single page, his method being to pick up a book, riffle through it, and decide whether or not it was worthy of his time. If the answer was affirmative, he would immediately set about mastering its essence so as to claim it as his own (years later he would write, "When I read a book, I throw it at my feet").

Out of the hundreds of books he went through in this fashion, he would select three favorites: Eric Hoffer's *The True Believer* (1951), because it showed the frailty of the American mind when it came to creative and autonomous thinking; Ortega y Gassett's *The Revolt of the Masses* (1930), because it showed the price that is paid when individuality is subverted by collective and politicized bargaining; and Niccolò Machiavelli's *The Prince*, because it presented with elegant precision the techniques necessary to dominate and turn in the right direction less fortunate minds.

Although each of these thinkers had seen deeply into a piece of the problem, none was able to offer a solution; and the more Tony pondered what he increasingly referred to as the "problem of civilization," the more he wondered if somehow his own as yet undeclared mission in life might be implicated in the answer.

At this juncture, a week before his twenty-first birthday, while lying in bed and sipping on a bottle of beer (as Tony would tell it), he found the answer to the problem of civilization, and to the problem of what to do with the rest of his life in a unifying, visionary flash of almost mystical insight. It was a vision that he would forever tinker with but never relinquish, and it would shape the remainder of his life. Ten years later, when he described it to his first disciple (Matthew), struggling to convey the magical power it originally held for him while admitting how much further he had developed it since then, he would lament, "I know it sounds simple now, but that was the key idea that started it all."

This was the visionary idea: Tony, a devotee of Americana and of the Civil War, had been thinking about all that Abraham Lincoln had done when it suddenly occurred to him that great as Lincoln's accomplishment undoubtedly was, it had been at best only a symbol. Lincoln's true longing, expressed as a passion to reunite North and South, was really to heal the deeper division in the heart of Americans, who were beginning, as the industrial revolution was picking up pace in the North, to move steadily away from their quintessential grass-roots frontierism. The real Civil War, as Tony suddenly understood, had been and still was being fought between the yearning for a life located in the land, with roots, and technological progress. And with that realization came the answer to his problem: for while technological advance was, of course, unstoppable, neither could it ever quell the longing in the hearts of Americans if that longing were really to turn backward to the grassroots and purity of spirit that had inspired the original founding fathers.

It meant returning, if not to the actuality, then to the symbols of the first Americans. Tony knew that by today's standards, from the standpoint of politics, that could sound like anarchy, but he wasn't afraid of being radical and he had no use for politics. He would begin by building small villages, enclaves within the heartland of the country, pointing to an America reborn. Perhaps men would all be armed, wear the clothes of frontiersmen, and even participate in symbolic adventures. *Symbolic* was a key word to Tony, since—recognizing that he had no political power and would never aspire to it—in order to achieve what he wanted to do, it was necessary that he speak directly, with archetypal force, to the unconscious mind of Americans, and therefore crucial that he choose his symbols with exquisite care. That was what he did, over the next ten years—he lovingly dwelt on the details of his Utopian American Villages that he dreamed would one day come to pass—but in that first ecstatic moment, when he jumped from his bed and began wildly pacing through his apartment, as Nietzsche had done before him while composing *Thus Spake Zarathustra*, it was enough that he had found his vision, and his mission, of an America reborn.

The transformation it brought about in him was little short of amazing. Just seven days later, in time for his twenty-first birthday, he had evolved from a splendid lone wolf, a mere master seducer of women and charismatic star salesman, to one worthy of the epithet "great man." In fact, Tony rapidly came to believe that he was perhaps the greatest man since Abraham Lincoln: where Lincoln had freed the slaves, he would liberate the spirit of all disheartened Americans imprisoned in a technological age. He now felt sorry for his philosophical antecedents, grassroots philosophers such as Eric Hoffer, men who had seen the problem but could not find the answer. He felt sorry for protest groups such as the John Birch Society, who believed that the emergence of political conservatism was the antidote for the palpable American malaise. He felt sorry for the Minutemen, who believed the way to salvation lay in greater military preparedness, and he felt sorry for the Ayn Randites, who were banking on a philosophical endorsement of empowered selfishness to purchase their happiness. Most of all, he felt sorry for the libertarians, whose politics, or absence of it, came closest to his own, but who lacked the philosophical scope of his Utopian vision.

As befitted his new-found crystal-clear sense of his own destiny and the path he must travel, he began making changes in his life. Resolving that a philosopher as important as he should not work at anything as degrading as selling industrial chemicals, he quit the job at which he had been making a small fortune and used the money he had saved to found the Tony West Company, a firm committed to the development and dissemination of original motivational tapes, devised by the master himself. Tony West was the first of a series of grandiose-sounding aliases he would experiment with, to convey a more appropriate sense of his historical identity, and the Tony West Company over the years lived up to its higher calling by continuously prospering. From motivational tapes he branched out to lectures, and finally, most lucrative of all, to seminars delivered to management executives on how to achieve the greatest mileage from their sales forces.

Onstage or in the conference room, he was a dazzling figure, the personification, with his indomitable smile and magical self-assurance, of the consummately motivated salesman who is the darling of every corporate executive. And his tapes and seminars worked well enough to keep his customers happy and asking for more: worked well enough to enable him to hire an interior decorator to further beautify his loft apartment in a style suitable to a man who one day would be regarded as a latter-day philosopher king. For Tony did not doubt or forget that he was a creative genius with a mission, and when he was not lecturing or selling in order to make money, or drinking beer or seducing women for pleasure, he was laboring with characteristic perseverance on what would be his philosophical magnum opus: a thousand-page work delving into a host of subjects but converging upon a fundamental focal point: the necessity for erecting Utopian American Neo-Frontier Villages.

Over the years, Tony would show parts of what he had written, and finally all of it, to carefully selected contacts in the publishing world culled from his business affiliations, who, while varying in the details of their opinion, were unanimous in their rejection; they either found him interesting in his radical eccentricity but "out of touch" with the mind-set of his contemporaries, or too "didactic," too "pompous," or too "moralistic."

After ten years of such uniform nonreceptivity to what he considered his finest and best ideas, Tony, who refused to allow himself to feel defeated, concluded that perhaps it was not meant to be, perhaps it was part of his destiny to be discovered after his death, like other great philosophers before him. It was one of those face-saving rationalizations on the grand scale in which he was fond of indulging, as, for example, his frequent assertion that the reason he had not gotten married, in spite of his surplus of adoring girlfriends, was attributable to his passion for philosophy and the fact that philosophers, historically, had been mainly bachelors.

It was a comfort to him, then, at the age of thirty, stoically to sigh that he was ahead of his time—but it was a rebirth shortly thereafter, when Tony received what he would reckon as the second greatest idea in his life. And it was all so simple. Why not use what was clearly his principal asset—the electric force of his personality—to propagate his ideas? Instead of fruitlessly searching for the correct philosophical symbols, which he would strain to capture in the most compelling literary style he could muster, why not actualize his ideas in flesh and blood, and use the dramatic showmanship in which he was already proficient to present them?

For the first time he envisioned seeking and gaining converts, proselytizing, gathering around himself a committed band of followers; and while he considered politics to be beneath him, the idea of being seen as the founder of a religious sect, such as the Black Muslims, was immensely appealing. On philosophical grounds he was an atheist, but on aesthetic, and especially Machiavellian, grounds, he regarded religion as the prime mover of men's minds, and therefore to be incorporated into the blueprint of his Utopian American Villages in the shape of appropriate religious ceremonies and rites that he would design, and that would reflect the expansionist spirit of the first Americans, which he wished to rekindle. Because he infinitely preferred a hedonistic to a puritanical lifestyle, he decided that the religion he would espouse would be a glorified paganism, a kind of Viking adventurousness, to symbolize the American longing for the lost frontier. It dawned on him that what he was contemplating was tantamount to founding a cult; and although fully aware that historically no cult had ever entered the mainstream of American consciousness, he accepted the challenge with unquestioning confidence. The name he chose for it was the Frontiersmen.

Such was the persona I was meant to take in, as it had been presented to Matthew by Tony, as it had been subsequently experienced and seen through Matthew's eyes, and as it had then been remembered and recreated for my benefit. Only when he was satisfied that I had been adequately tutored, about a month after I had first met him, did Matthew finally tell me the circumstances of his initial meeting with Tony.

The meeting had been arranged by Conrad, his older brother, who was an old friend of Tony's, and who had slowly succumbed to mounting pressure to set up the introduction. Suspicious by nature, Conrad could not help wondering why, after all these years, Tony was suddenly so anxious to meet his kid brother, and he felt obliged to forewarn Matthew that while undoubtedly brilliant, dynamic, entertaining, and "a character," Tony was never to be fully trusted, was a user, the most conceited man he had ever met, perhaps even a bit of a megalomaniac.

Taking note, as he always did, of what Conrad had told him, his guard therefore up, but intrigued as to why someone of such reputed accomplishment should be eager to meet an eighteen-year-old high-school graduate, Matthew first encountered Tony Patrano on a street corner in mid-Manhattan. As Matthew would remember:

"Right from the start, he was different from anyone I had ever met. What everyone else was interested in didn't concern him. He had his own agenda. We went to an automat for lunch and—this impressed me—pointing to the cheese sandwich he was eating, he commented, 'Look at this. Fast processed food. People are in such a hurry to make money so as to purchase the next materialistic possession that they are willing to put junk into their bodies.'

"Puzzled, I asked what he thought was wrong with that, and what he thought people should be doing instead, and without batting an eye, he replied, 'Trying to be great. Trying to make something of their lives that might stand the test of time, that they might be proud to see portrayed as a work of art, on the stage.'

"I had never met anyone who talked like that, who took life so seriously, as though he had a standard of values, a philosophy of life, that was higher than other people's. It wasn't that he was pompous or heavy; as a matter of fact, although he rarely joked, there was usually an ironic or sardonic note to almost everything he said. 'Absurdity' was probably his favorite word, and I really came to believe, soon after I met him, that he had a special talent for uncovering the unsuspected absurdity of things most people took for granted. At the very least, when our lunch had ended, I felt that knowing him would be a kind of education I would not get elsewhere."

I asked Matthew if, in retrospect, he could see signs or omens of what was to come.

Matthew struggled with the question, fell silent, then:

"I'm an all-or-nothing person. Either I believe or I don't. Yes, there were things that bothered me about Tony from the beginning and made me want not to believe in him. He was more arrogant by a long shot than anyone I had ever seen or heard of, and it seemed absolutely necessary to him that he come out on top in any argument. This especially annoyed me because I'm that way myself, I like to win arguments, but I never could with Tony, and nobody else could either.

"It was also hard for me to accept that such a thing as Utopian American Villages could ever come to pass in my lifetime, and frankly, I was secretly hoping that they wouldn't. I hate politics, as it is, and the idea of being a part of a movement trying to lead people into founding a cult seemed just incredibly bizarre and frightening to me. So I would put it out of my mind."

When I asked Matthew what it was, then, that made him so loyal to Tony and such a believer in him, he no longer had to search for a reply.

"I loved his confidence. I didn't like his arrogance, but I loved his confidence. It amazed me that nothing seemed to shake him up. He reminded me of what they used to say about Muhammad Ali: that he never blinked in the ring. It wasn't just that he always had a comeback for whatever you said or did, he had a *terrific* comeback.

"I'll give you an example. High school was easy for me, so I used to spend a lot of my time reading. I estimated that I had read more books than most of my teachers, more books by far than any of my classmates, and I had a reputation for being not only a 'brain' but a phenomenal scholar as well, especially for my age. Still, any book I mentioned Tony had not only read but had formulated a well-thought-out opinion about. And sometimes he had even incorporated it into his philosophy.

"Now here's my example, and there were many of them. I had just read for the first time about gestalt psychology, and was fascinated, and trying to understand the idea of the whole being greater than the sum of the parts. I mentioned it to Tony, and nodding, he instantly replied, in that unhurried way of his, 'It's really simple, Matthew. Just imagine for a moment two halves of a key, which are separated. Now put them together, mentally. Of course the key, when you think of it this way, as the sum of its two halves, immediately has a new function—it can unlock a door—which it did not have before, but that is only because, as a whole, it now has a new relationship (not a new part) to the external world. Therefore, everything the gestalt psychologists say can be boiled down and explained by this brief formula: The whole equals the sum of the parts plus the new relationship that the whole now has to the world.' "

Only a god, or so it seemed to Matthew, could speak so fluently on nearly every subject; in the succeeding months, as he spent more and more time with and put more and more questions to his new mentor, he began to think that perhaps Tony, like Muhammad Ali before him, although unquestionably arrogant, was similarly speaking the truth: that beneath the flamboyant and incessant bragging, was the cold fact that he *was* the greatest, an important philosopher, a genius, as he claimed, and even a man with a message and an historical destiny to fulfill.

It was the historical destiny part that worried Matthew, but as long as it was relegated to the future and remained sufficiently unspecified so as to be murky, he could handle it; and five months later, after they had become inseparable friends, when Tony anointed him the first disciple of the Frontiersmen, he nervously but proudly accepted the honor. The tremendous flattery and attention being bestowed upon him by the most charismatic person he had ever met was a gift he could not refuse, and as for the service, for the favor of being named first disciple, he might one day be called upon to perform, it seemed comfortably far off.

Yet it would be sooner than Matthew thought; he was beginning to realize that the closer he grew to Tony, the greater were the demands that would be made upon him. Chief of these was that Matthew assist him in recruiting further disciples, and when he registered for his freshman year at Washington Square College, he experienced for the first time just how insistent and bullying his mentor would be, for Tony was relentless in his efforts to persuade Matthew to arrange introductions with likely prospects (likely according to Tony, who interrogated him on every new acquaintance).

It was the kind of proselytizing that Matthew, who prided himself on being a shy, introverted, bookish loner, particularly hated, but felt obligated to do, as well as pressured into doing, as payment for the friendship he increasingly depended on, the fuss Tony continued to make over him, and the endless hours of freewheeling philosophizing, which he especially loved. Yet the more Matthew spoke about his relationship with Tony, the more he was forced to accept the nature of his conflict; on the one hand, he felt retrospectively swindled, manipulated, and cheated of everything that had been promised to him; on the other hand, he was still susceptible to a nostalgic longing for the idealistic friendship he had once fervently believed in.

It helped Matthew to reconcile the two, to articulate more freely, without fear of reprisal, what until now had lurked in the back of his mind as a dimly felt undercurrent: and it aided in the exorcism of his erstwhile mentor for him to vocalize again and again his long-smoldering criticism. He could never, for example, understand why a man as brilliant as Tony needed to be so childishly, boastfully competitive, to see all things in terms of a contest in which he would unfailingly (and belligerently, if he had to) declare himself the winner. Matthew resented it that not only did he find it necessary always to defeat him, but that he was also required to be audience and yes-man to some of the most outrageous bragging he had ever heard: that he had once "come thirteen times in a row with the same woman, which was a world record"; that he had solved a famous brainteaser in about an hour an half less than the minimum allotted time, which was also "probably a world record"; and that since, as he believed, boxing was more a matter of motivation and determination than athletic ability, his own natural punching power "was probably on a par with Rocky Marciano's."

Although Mathew had often been baited into engaging in playfully competitive arm-punching contests with Tony and could attest to how hard he punched, he had no doubt that had Rocky Marciano been around, Marciano would have punched substantially harder. He could live with his mentor's comic braggadocio and write it off as the quirkiness of the great man, but he could not dismiss what he felt was the dark side of Tony.

This dark side frightened Matthew because, in its blatant irrationality, it seemed to put into question everything Tony supposedly stood for. By blatant irrationality Matthew meant a certain diabolical sadism that gave him "the chills," and when asked for an example, he explained:

"He liked to refer to himself as a 'man of good will,' but he also wanted it known that he was extremely hard, and could do whatever was necessary in order to advance his cause. On a number of occasions he would say, perfectly seriously, 'I could pull the trigger on anyone and sleep like a baby the following night.' It seemed that he was justifying murder on philosophical and moral grounds, but I could never accept that he could be capable of such a thing. I explained it by pointing to his mother: Tony loved the fact that his foster mother was a hot-headed Sicilian with a wild and fearless temper who, as he frankly admitted, 'scared the pants off me as a kid'; and I told myself that boasting that he could 'out-hit' a hit man was Tony's way of competing with his mother and with men, whom he fondly referred to as 'comical gangsters.'

"I dealt with his claims that he could be a mafioso murderer, if he had to be, the same way I dealt with his plans to create Utopian American Villages—by pushing them way into the future. I told myself that if anything really bad was going to happen, and if I was forced to be a part of it, as I was afraid I would be, then it was going to be so far in the future that I didn't have to worry.

"But I couldn't do that with the past, when it came to certain stories, 'revenge' stories, which Tony insisted on telling, and which my brother corroborated. Nothing bothered me more and gave me such creeps as when he would tell me what had happened to Michael, a former friend, who according to Tony had betrayed him. There were few things that so infuriated him as betrayal, and he would go to fantastic lengths to concoct the perfect Machiavellian revenge. It reminded me of Room 101 in Orwell's *1984*, the room where you go to find out what it is you are most terrified of.

"In Michael's case, what he was most terrified of was that Jane, his long-term girlfriend, would sleep with another man behind his back. So Tony arranged for a secret videotape, courtesy of an electronics expert friend, of his orgiastic seduction of Jane, which included, among other things, her recorded confession of how sexually unappealing she had always found Michael. He then made a special trip to a bank to procure thirty silver dollars, meant to symbolically represent the thirty pieces of silver for which Judas betrayed Christ, and together with the pornographically explicit videotaped seduction of his girlfriend, express-mailed them to Michael.

"Maybe because I refused to believe that anything could possible justify such sadism, I asked Tony for the details of Michael's 'betrayal.' To my amazement he was not only unclear about but uninterested in the specifics of the offense. It had something to do with something Michael had said behind his back to mutual friends, showing unquestionable disrespect for what he stood for, and that was enough for Tony. What did interest him was gloating about the spectacular disarray in which his bombshell of an express-mail package had left Michael, and when he moved away from New York just a few months later, Tony wanted the credit for it. It was a story I unfortunately heard him tell many times, which he would always refer to as 'my masterpiece of Machiavellian revenge.'

"I used to wonder if Tony was giving me a not-too-subtle message about what would be in store for me should I ever cross him. Not only did I intend never to cross him, but I took pride in being an absolutely loyal friend. It hurt me and scared me, therefore, that Tony might be threatening me. But what scared me the most was what he had done to Michael—which I could never understand, and of course never respect."

Matthew made sure that he stayed on the right side of Tony by developing in spite of himself into an efficient talent scout who could quickly spot a malleable young mind and suavely engineer an introduction with his mentor. Tony did the rest, and over the next two years the team of Matthew and Tony, of first disciple and founder, worked astonishingly well, accounting for ten new disciples. By Matthew's inventory, these were: Stuart, a swarthy, muscular philosophy student, who boasted that he had once gunned down a charging black bear in the Adirondack Mountains, when only an eighteen-year-old; Sean, an elegantly mannered poker-faced musician who loved to entertain by performing on the piano simultaneous improvisations of his two heroes, Cole Porter and Wolfgang Mozart; Ted, a somber student of computer science who wondered if he might have the makings of a poet; Julian, a jovial but passionate student of economics who openly adored power; Glen, a lean, rakishly handsome self-proclaimed screw-up, who was intent on defying and making life miserable for his Establishment father, who was a renowned brain surgeon; Jay, a manifestly troubled, apparently schizoid, but idiosyncratically amusing aspiring young playwright who liked to expostulate in the style of his literary mentor, Edward Albee; Betty, Tony's girlfriend for the previous two years, ever since she had migrated from the Far West and her Mormon family, who freely confessed that she wished to dedicate the remainder of her life to furthering her lover's cause; Emma, a depressed bohemian college dropout, who recently had become the latest in Tony's string of girlfriends and who seemed never to leave his side; Bobby, a regularly employed television actor, who, next to Tony, was the most financially well off; and Cliff, an irrepressible Irish comic, talented enough to have been a professional impressionist, who could uncannily impersonate most of his friends, as well as scores of celebrities, and who functioned as the cult clown.

Of the eleven disciples, Stuart, who was twenty-two, was the oldest. Matthew liked them all, and if only because he enjoyed the special status of being the first and the one closest to Tony, he was well regarded by them. Increasingly thinking of them as more than friends, more than family, it dawned on him that this tiny unknown group had become without doubt the most important people on earth to him.

And they wouldn't be unknown for long, if Tony had anything to do with it. Ecstatic that in just two years he could gather around him eleven committed disciples, he decided to mark what he considered perhaps *the* most significant milestone in his life with a simple ceremony. It was a ritual completely designed by Tony, and it signaled the beginning of a pattern wherein Tony more and more would seek to record, in the form of dramatically meaningful symbols, the events in his life that he deemed historic.

So they convened, at Tony's command, in a luxurious two-tier executive suite in the Statler Hilton Hotel. The date was June 10, 1979, the end of a decade and the birth of a new spirit. Standing before a lectern, equipped with a microphone and a tape recorder, Tony began by announcing that he was officially founding the Cult of the Frontiersmen, and he continued to speak extemporaneously, without written cues, for the next three hours.

Never had Matthew, who had probably spent thousands of hours conversing with and listening to Tony, ever heard anything like this: ranging over a decade of philosophical thinking and writing, occasionally pausing for scintillating digression, synthesizing with effortless skill, it was a performance that not only dazzled but bewitched the audience.

That was the good news. The downside was that Matthew knew that what he had dreaded from the start, what he devoutly wished he might never have to face, was at hand: with the inception of the cult, the utopian ideas of Tony Patrano would be transferred from the realm of abstraction and the drawing board of the imagination into a reality, however unbelievable. It meant that the tempo of events would be automatically speeded up; and while Matthew's presentiments proved valid, he was relieved to discover that along with the increase in tempo, the level of daily excitement and stimulation would be correspondingly raised.

The next year following the inauguration of the Cult of the Frontiersmen, in comparison with the preceding years, seemed as if it were being lived on fast forward. More and more Matthew, although he retained his status as right-hand man, had the disquieting feeling that what he said and thought no longer mattered nearly as much, as it had at first, and that he was slowly being shoved into the background. The influx of ten additional disciples had done more than attenuate his previous importance, it had radically metamorphosed what in Matthew's eyes had been a basically satisfying, philosophically noble, one-on-one buddy relationship into a comparatively anonymous role in a supposedly history-making cult. Despite the undeniable increase in fun and adventurousness, Matthew preferred what to him had been the good old days; and he noted with resentment, disdain, and then jealousy the alteration in Tony's personality, which he attributed to the formation of the cult.

First of all, whereas Tony on occasion had always been insufferably arrogant, there was now a kind of magisterial, grandiose quality—as though Tony, as historical missionary leader, was entitled to exemptions that ordinary mortals were not—that Matthew had never seen before. Suddenly he remembered the premonition of his brother, Conrad, who had warned him that Tony had a bit of megalomania in him.

Sometimes it seemed more than a bit, as Matthew bitterly concluded he was faced with a new Tony, who no longer bothered to apologize for outbursts of temper or to sweeten his demands, which continued to mount, with negotiable concessions, who acted as though he expected his requests, however exacting, to be granted, not for personal gain, but always for the cause.

And increasingly, whatever Tony said was the cause, *became* the cause. When he said it was necessary, as the founder of a hedonist cult, to have multiple girlfriends—and accordingly insisted on having Betty and Emma simultaneously attend every group function—then *that* was the cause. When he exhorted the new disciples, as earnestly as he had exhorted Mathew before them, to pass the word to their friends that a genius with an important philosophy was in their midst, then *that* was the cause, and when he grew incensed should anyone fail to address him by the pseudonym he had chosen (Tony West), somehow that was on account of, and on behalf of, the cause.

In what seemed a whirlwind meteoric year following the birth of the cult, there were two things that Matthew especially hated. The first was what struck him as an ill-advised plan of Tony's to pretest the public's receptiveness to his philosophy by trying to crack the college lecture circuit with unsolicited doses of his ideas, cleverly "packaged" as engagingly provocative intellectual rebelliousness. And this entailed an assortment of cult members, including Matthew, standing up before selected metropolitan collegiate audiences—mustered through the tireless distribution of mimeographed flyers—and discoursing tongue-in-cheek upon the consciousness-raising joy of life in a cult.

Not surprisingly, college audiences who had never seen anything quite like this before—so out of sync with any political, civil rights, or social issue currently being debated, so disdainfully futuristic—did not know what to make of it. At New York University, in a disappointingly middle-sized classroom, a smattering of bemused students alternately heckled, chuckled, or searched in vain for a personal connection to this talk about Utopian American Villages. At Brooklyn College, in a huge auditorium, unexpectedly packed, puzzled students were more or less deferential toward something they clearly did not understand but perhaps felt obligated to check out in case it eventually proved intellectually respectable. At St. John's University, in an overflowing but diminutive classroom, a few brave students, in a spirit of fun, elected to propose alternative American Utopian Villages, and thereby debate Tony, who—loving the opportunity to engage in spontaneous one-on-one competition—was probably at his best: so much so that when it was over, the priest who had consented to the lecture, obviously tickled at the student response and jovially clapping Tony on the shoulder, announced, "Come back any time, boys!" And at Queens College, in yet another gigantic auditorium, an unruly crowd of agitated students, seemingly convinced that the term "Utopian American Village" was a euphemism and a buzzword for an incipient neo-Nazi movement in their midst, repeatedly interrupted the lectures with cries of "fascist," nearly precipitating a mini-riot. While at City College, in a welcome (to Matthew) contrast, in an undersized dingy classroom, only three students showed up, none of whom bothered to stay until the end.

Much as he hated standing in front of college audiences, obediently delivering his prepared lecture, which lasted no more than five minutes and had been deliberately constructed by Matthew so as to be safely obscure, he could somehow get through that. If he felt like a "puppet and a jackass" trying to pass himself off before college students his own age as the first disciple of an historic cult destined to represent the wave of the future, he could comfort himself that at least he had not committed the egregious gaffe Tony had: he had not seriously miscalculated the effects of his ideas once they were transposed from the one-on-one proselytizing encounters, at which Tony was an undoubted master, to the broader public arena of the college lecture circuit, where they quickly fizzled and became ineffectual.

But what he could not tolerate, what he felt might stretch him to the breaking point, was his compulsory enrollment into what he sarcastically referred to as "Tony's army of carpenters."

Whether it was because he prided himself on being an intellectually passionate, reclusive, scholarly (except for the cult activities), and decidedly nonmanual person, or because he bitterly objected to having to prove his loyalty by performing menial labor, this new project was something he refused to fathom. It would never make sense to him that Tony insisted, was apparently obsessed with the idea, that the twelve of them should build, essentially with their own hands, a symbolic cult clubhouse in a huge vacated loft area leased by Tony on Houston Street, near Chinatown.

Yet that is what they did. For nearly ten months, beginning soon after the memorable inauguration of the cult in the executive suite in the Statler Hilton Hotel, they toiled and sweated alongside their philosopher-king foreman, who tirelessly supervised and exhorted them to finish their historic haunt. At Tony's behest, they installed runners in the ceiling to accommodate sliding walls, laid down wall-to-wall carpeting, inserted a frontier-style mahogany bar replete with inverted barrel chairs, and added a sprinkling of futons in preparation for the orgies predicted by Tony (and dreaded by Matthew). Finally, at his own expense—perhaps to set a tone of conspiratorial secrecy he considered necessary—he had most of the sprawling loft area soundproofed.

Inside the clubhouse Matthew found little intrigue and even less philosophy, and continued to be preoccupied with what he considered the ongoing personality changes in Tony. No longer even attempting to gloss over the contradictions that had always been present in his character, Tony simply did what he wanted to, as though the fact that he had founded an historic cult was a justification so global that it could sanction anything and everything. Thus, if he wanted to sleep with Betty in the mornings and Emma in the evenings, he did so, without explanations. If he wanted to hang a gigantic poster of Abraham Lincoln on a clubhouse sliding wall, he did so; and if he decided to hang a second poster of his favorite actor, Clint Eastwood, he did so without bothering to repeat his familiar joking rationale, "I know he's an intellectual lightweight, and he can't act, but at least he's *trying* to be an early American Frontiersman."

What most disturbed Matthew, so far as Tony's personality was concerned, was what seemed to him the exponential increase in his competitive boastfulness. Much of the mandatory clubhouse meetings revolved around contests dreamed up by Tony, which invariably pitted one man against another and allegedly were intended to test the individual pioneering mettle of each of the disciples. Over and above the traditional arm-punching contests (to test grit), there were dramatic reading contests (to determine who was the most effective speaker), philosophy interpretation contests (to determine who had the best mind), drinking contests (to determine who had the greatest Rabelaisian lust for life), and an endless assortment of fun-and-games contests (to determine who was the best all-around competitor), Tony's personal favorite being knife-throwing contests and "drawing" contests (using a stopwatch to record who could pull a pistol from a holster fastest).

To Matthew, the contests were not only transparent excuses and wire-drawn setups engineered to show that Tony could win at anything, but in a sense they were over before they began: although Tony regularly, and lustily, competed, the implicit assumption was that as acknowledged champion he was doing so only for sport, and that the true purpose of the competition was to determine who was *second* best. And it rankled Matthew that one of the numerous changes that had arisen in his relationship with his mentor since the inauguration of the cult was that now— instead of its being taken for granted that as right-hand man he was automatically in second place—he found himself forced to fight for his spot in the cult pecking order.

Therefore, in spite of nagging guilt that he was reacting with less than absolute loyalty, he was not terribly sorry, or terribly shocked, when the dream of the clubhouse-as-historic-sanctuary suddenly collapsed. Although it had been barely three years since his brother had introduced him on a street corner in mid-Manhattan to his charismatic friend, Matthew had already chronicled what to him were a series of inexplicable reversals of plans; and he was by far the least surprised of the assembled disciples when Tony, standing before the clubhouse lectern, abruptly announced that, just two months after its completion, he had decided to abandon it.

When asked what would then happen to the clubhouse they had just built, Tony shrugged, "We'll tear it down," and when asked where they would next be going to hold their meetings, Tony, with a dramatic smile, revealed, "We're going to California!"

Although there is said to be a fine line between drug dependency and drug addiction, between severe borderline personality and psychosis, it is still one person who crosses over—not one person who, in a kind of psychological mitosis, splits cleanly into two distinct personalities (a favorite perception of recovered addicts, who often divide their mental life into a pre-addictive and an addictive psyche). When I tried to make this point to Matthew—who, taken by the irrationality and seeming loss of contact with reality of the California version of Tony, would emphasize how utterly alien that was to the pre-California, more rational Tony—he became more angry than I had seen him. Apparently it was important to him that the Tony who precipitously tore down the clubhouse and migrated to California with yet another dream of reaching the people through the magic of the entertainment industry was not the charismatic philosopher he had once known and admired. Exactly when the radical change in personality and break with reality had occurred, Matthew was not sure, but there had definitely been a number of disturbing signs or omens leading up to what Matthew would subsequently designate as "the first big trauma."

Perhaps the first such omen was recorded, with poetic justice, not by Matthew but by Conrad, who had a well-deserved reputation for detecting chinks in someone's characterological armor far in advance of anyone else; and who was making his first official visit to California in order to see both his friend and his brother. At the time Conrad had been no more than normally worried about what he considered his younger brother's excessive involvement with the activities of the cult, chalking that up, as well as the recent move to California, to the latest antics of his brilliant, erratic friend—but that would change soon after the visit.

As Conrad confided to Matthew many months later, when Matthew had returned in a state of panic to New York City, he had heard something he would never forget—something that Matthew, much to his brother's alarm, had deluded himself into thinking was just one more example of Tony's harmless braggadocio—that his new plan was to become President of the United States within two years. And it was not even what Tony had said, fantastic though it sounded, but the circumstances and manner in which he had said it, that had so disturbed Conrad. For while they were sitting in the living room of the pleasant two-story wooden house, laughing and drinking beer as they watched William F. Buckley Jr. elegantly debating on TV, Tony had announced out of the blue, "Someday, when I'm President of the United States, he's going to be forced to have me on his program, and it'll be a piece of cake. I'll destroy him."

At first Conrad was puzzled: not once in the ten years he had known Tony had he heard a whisper of political ambition, let alone aspiration to the Presidency, and he could only stammer, "When you're President of the United States?"

It was the opportunity to mystify and spook—first by making an outrageous statement and then defiantly, exuberantly, and brilliantly defending it—that Tony loved, except that this time he was apparently serious. Tilting back superciliously in his chair, he solemnly outlined his most recent plan: in the midst of the remarkable political ascendancy of Ronald Reagan, the time must be ripe for a man of such superior motivational and demagogic skills as he possessed. It meant abandoning the minor-league college lecture circuit and moving into the "big time" of

Machiavellian politics. It meant utilizing his philosophical and dramatic genius to produce a series of innocent-looking, commercially appealing screenplays that would contain powerful subliminal messages associated with the idea of Utopian American Villages. That was Phase One of the strategy, designed to make Tony West and his band of followers famous in the entertainment industry. Phase Two would be the consolidation of this power base, by whatever Machiavellian means necessary (in the manner of Ronald Reagan), into a political foothold that would lead inexorably to the Presidency of the United States.

The explanation plunged Conrad deeper into confusion, and as though to give his friend one last chance to redeem his credibility, he asked, "But how can you be so *sure*?"

"I'm sure," replied Tony, and indeed never in ten years had Conrad seen him so absolutely, serenely convinced of anything.

And six hours later, waiting in the lounge of the Los Angeles airport for his return flight to New York City, the true explanation, which until now had painfully eluded him, suddenly exploded in his mind. It was all so horrifyingly simple. Conrad rushed to telephone his wife, Jennifer, the one person with whom he shared all his epiphanies.

"Tony's crazy, he's gone crazy!" Conrad would remember that he had been crying as he spoke to his wife, heartbroken at the realization that what he had been witnessing was perhaps the ruin of a close friend's brilliant mind, yet simultaneously and curiously uplifted as a new sense of purpose dramatically unfolded to him: he must at any cost rescue his impressionable younger brother from the dangerous influence of a man who, he was certain, had irreversibly crossed the line that separates artistic and philosophical eccentricity from madness.

For Matthew, unfortunately, there would be no such epiphany, only signs and omens, which he easily discredited, being much too busy and swept up in the excitement and changes brought about by the move to California. Part of the grand plan was for it to take place in two waves. The first wave, a kind of scouting expedition, was composed of Tony; his girlfriend Betty; Matthew, still his right-hand man; the television actor, Bobby, now considered vital as a link to the targeted entertainment industry; Sean, the dilettante musician; and Jay, the idiosyncratic playwright, both of whom gladly volunteered for what they regarded as an attractive, can't-miss adventure. Left behind were Emma, Tony's most recent girlfriend, and the remaining disciples, with the instructions to look after things in New York City and await the signal to join them in California.

Although that first scouting party included only six people, Tony, his eye on the future and thinking more grandiosely than ever, secured the lease not to just one but to three separate two-story houses, straddling Cienega Avenue, which a few blocks away bisected Wilshire Boulevard in the business section of Los Angeles. And like an invading conquering general distributing his spoils, he allocated one house entirely to Matthew and Bobby, another to Sean and Jay, and a third to Betty and himself.

No doubt in Tony's mind the houses would soon be brimming with disciples and friends of disciples, both new and old, but for Matthew it was more than enough, in the first few months following their arrival in Los Angeles, to try to take in and digest such a change in his customary lifestyle. At least that was what he told himself, and that was how he managed to discount most of the creeping changes in Tony's personality that he could not fail to notice. One such change that he could not successfully ignore, and that would constitute what Matthew would later allude to as the first principal omen that something was really wrong with his friend, concerned the woman whom Tony had allocated to the second wave and temporarily left behind, Emma. Up until that memorable incident, Matthew could not even remember Tony so much as acknowledging that he was experiencing the slightest trouble handling a woman, let alone displaying unmistakable and embarrassing signs of romantic distress.

Yet, as they sat chatting, in what had become a daily morning ritual, on the front-porch steps of Tony's house, which was situated about fifty yards down the block from his own house, that is exactly what Matthew saw. Suddenly Tony, who had been talking, almost whispering, in an uncharacteristically hoarse voice about how Emma had been suspiciously resisting his request to join him in California, slumped forward. To his astonishment, Matthew observed his friend, face in hands, begin first to cry and then to heave with sobs.

He could not believe it: Tony West, the self-styled Don Juan, founder of an historic cult, actually weeping over the unhappy outcome of a supposedly trivial love affair! So great was Matthew's incredulity that he could scarcely pay attention to Tony's moaning recital of what he believed to be the damning evidence, all pointing to Emma's imminent betrayal of him. How never before had Emma crossed him. How increasingly she had been telling Tony, on the long-distance telephone, in a confused way about her old friend, Steven Schultz, who was unexpectedly pressing her to begin "dating" him and abandon this foolish, self-destructive idea of joining her "crackpot bigamous lover" in California. How Emma didn't know what to do, had been miserable for a long time over being forced to participate in a competition with another woman, and wanted the reassurance, should she go to the trouble of moving to California, that she would be able to look forward to the security of being at least number one girlfriend (she knew better than to dare insist on faithfulness).

Rational as such an ultimatum might seem, Tony experienced it as a profound narcissistic injury, and, face still buried in his hands, he bitterly calculated his options. Matthew, who had enough trouble finding and maintaining one girlfriend, could offer little solace and less advice, although he tried, to a man torn between two lovers. Besides, his heart was scarcely in it; he continued to be morbidly preoccupied with the first clear example of behavior that, he felt certain, could be described as neurotic. In view of Tony's longstanding denigration of psychoanalysis and psychiatry ("they see people as essentially disgusting"), his patronizing dismissal even of Freud ("perhaps he was a minor genius"), and his unqualified contempt for the weakness of people who enter psychotherapy, Matthew recognized that this was an important if rebellious insight, and therefore not likely to be popular with Tony.

So Matthew, who could not resist expressing it to his friend who sat by his side on the porch steps with undeniable traces of tears sparkling in his eyes, made what he hoped would be received as an unprovocative joke: "Hey, Tony, don't tell me *you're* finally becoming neurotic!"

Still looking quite pale and shaken, not bothering to mask his depression, and apparently unable or uninterested in trying to recover from his display of uncharacteristic vulnerability by bluffing (his typical stratagem), Tony smiled sheepishly, rose from his seat on the porch, and disappeared into the house. Although he was gone for a good hour, Matthew guessed that was the time required on the phone to New York to iron out the differences between himself and Emma; and when Tony reemerged, his huge grin seemed to substantiate the intuition.

"Emma's coming in a week," chirped Tony, unmysteriously in high spirits. "I'm moving her in with Sean and Jay."

Edging closer to Matthew, and whispering conspiratorially in his ear (another "sign" that would be repeated in the succeeding weeks), he cautioned, "Betty doesn't know this yet," and then, in another of those dramatic surprises meant to spook people, which he dearly loved, he announced, "Two weeks later, everyone else is coming!"

It was the beginning of October 1980, as Matthew would recall; when he was composed enough to resist interrupting himself with outbursts of hysterical laughter, he liked to adopt the psychological pose of someone narrating the diary of a nightmare. The date was pivotal, because afterward the signs and omens leading up to what Matthew would subsequently designate as the "first big trauma" noticeably increased.

There were whole days, for example, shortly after Emma arrived, on schedule, where Tony would seem to disappear, sequestering himself in a solitary room with, alternately, Emma or Betty; incommunicado except for an occasional scream of frustrated rage at what he perceived as castrating resistance to his proposal for an amicable ménage à trois. What he eventually worked out, not to the satisfaction of either Betty or Emma, was that he would spend specified days of every week with each of them, in separate houses. After all, it was only making public and official what everyone knew he had been doing for many months—sleeping with one woman in the morning and another in the evening—and he attributed their strenuous opposition to a selfish disregard for the ordeal he was about to undergo.

That ordeal would be precipitated in a week by the arrival of the remaining New York disciples, the so-called second wave, that would complete the move to California. It therefore meant that Tony, as leader, had to be ready with a blueprint, a master plan (to justify the move) convincingly outlining a series of steps, that would make the Cult of the Frontiersmen, in time, deservedly famous and influential. Step One, as he had recently explained to Conrad, involved the production of commercially successful, but subliminally propagandist, screenplays. Now in another epiphany (the proliferation of which, in the coming week, Matthew would count as one more unmistakable sign of disturbance) Tony decided to enlist the services of Sean, Jay, Bobby, and Matthew, all of whom prided themselves on their creative potential, and to use that potential to further the cause. Besides, as Tony insisted, it would be *fun* (a justification he often used when he felt that what he was asking for might be taken as an extraordinary demand).

And in that final week, preceding the arrival of the second wave of disciples, there *was* a kind of desperate fun as Bobby, Sean, Jay, and himself would convene alternately in Emma's or Betty's living room for screenwriting brainstorming sessions superintended by an oddly ebullient Tony. But it was that other side, the corresponding dark side of his friend that even Matthew could not explain, that especially frightened him: times, for example, when Tony would not simply disappear into a single room with either Betty or Emma, but would completely vanish— as though he had executed a well-thought-out escape—and people from all three houses would one by one inquire as to the whereabouts of Tony.

During the countdown of days until the anticipated arrival of the New York disciples, an eerie feeling, which Matthew could not put his finger on, began to pervade the three houses. More and more Tony seemed subject to states of heightened emotion: elation, fear, rage, which not infrequently would translate into spells of furious activity. There was the day Tony retreated to his bedroom, specifying that absolutely no one was to disturb him, whereupon he spent hours on the long-distance telephone tying up the loose ends of a hastily convened farewell meeting of the disciples in the Statler Hilton Hotel. The meeting was meant to symbolize what to Tony was the historic migration of the Cult of the Frontiersmen to the West Coast, and apparently it was a highly secretive affair, each of the participants being sworn not to repeat what had transpired behind closed doors, even to their West Coast brothers (which they never did).

Such conspiratorial silence, obviously imposed by Tony, irked Matthew, but it did not bother him nearly as much as what would happen on the day just preceding the advent of the New York disciples, which he would subsequently designate as "the first big trauma." It began, inauspiciously enough, in the backyard of the third house, the only one on the opposite side of La Cienega Avenue, with an informal early-morning chat with Sean, the stylish musician, whose dry humor Matthew usually found entertaining. But on this occasion Sean seemed more anxious than he could remember him and uncharacteristically rattled.

"What do you think of what's going on up there?" Nervously whispering as though fearful he might be overheard, Sean jerked his head toward the second story of the house behind him.

Looking up, Matthew saw a bathroom window slightly opened, thought he heard singing or humming in a voice that was probably Tony's, but saw no significance in either observation.

"What is it?"

"He's taking a bath."

"A bath?" Matthew could recall Tony taking showers, but never a bath.

"Four or five times a day."

It dawned on Matthew that outside of spontaneously arranged get-togethers, he had of late seen precious little of Tony, who had been living in the same house with Sean, Jay, and Emma (it was her turn) for the past three days, and that perhaps Sean might therefore have something important to tell him. Suddenly he was a rapt listener, pressing Sean for further details.

"He just started taking these baths a couple of days ago. The day after he called that big mystery meeting in the Statler Hilton Hotel, I think. He was worried that he was sweating too much. He would mop his brow and say, 'My blood pressure must be a million degrees.'

"Then he would jump in the tub and sit there for a long time. Emma would bring him a fresh supply of cold compresses and sometimes sit on a chair by the side of the tub and hold them against his forehead. All the while he would be talking very fast about his ideas and plans through the open door to me or anyone else who was around."

Pausing for dramatic emphasis, Sean added, "I don't mind that he sometimes walks around the house naked, although I don't like it. But ... have you heard one of his hideous laughs?"

"Hideous laughs?"

"Yes."

A few nights ago, well into the evening, Matthew had heard what he thought was a scream, as though someone were in great pain or being beaten, which gradually subsided—but it did not remotely sound like a human laugh.

"This past Wednesday, around ten or eleven in the evening, I thought I heard someone scream."

Sean quickly nodded. "That's how it starts out, like a scream. Your bedroom is probably a hundred feet or more away, but you still heard it."

Even if Matthew could have taken such information in, there would not have been time to reflect upon it. When he returned to his own house, Bobby told him that Tony had telephoned with an urgent message: Everyone had to have the final plot outlines of his screenplay ready by eight o'clock that night, because there was going to be a big meeting in Tony's house concerning new plans, to take effect immediately after the arrival of the New York disciples. That left barely nine hours to produce an acceptable outline for a promising screenplay, and, sensing that Tony could not be expected to be rational should they fail to deliver, after a brief exchange of embarrassed glances, they hurried to their rooms.

As scheduled, the meeting took place in the spacious living room of the house that flanked the opposite side of La Cienega Avenue, where Tony was temporarily residing. They sat around a massive, antique-looking black table with Tony, shirtless, for some reason, at the head, Emma and Betty on either side, and Bobby, Jay, Sean, and Matthew at the far end. Although there was a gallon of Chablis wine (Tony's favorite drink since coming to California) and a supply of cups in the center of the table, the meeting was to be all business, with none of the sportive diversions that often lightened such gatherings. Tony, despite being only half dressed, somehow managed to look and act impressively formal, while Matthew, remembering his morning conversation with Sean, found himself scrutinizing Tony's brow for signs of sweat.

He saw none, but felt certain soon after the meeting began that something was wrong with Tony, who was unduly distracted (often pausing to stare intently through an adjacent window), short-tempered, and forgetful. He spoke at breakneck speed about what he envisioned lay directly ahead for the Cult of the Frontiersmen, but first, as he repeatedly stressed, sometimes wiping at his still sweatless brow, there was the matter of the screenplay outlines. And for about three hours Bobby, Sean, Jay, and Matthew in turn obediently recited their notes and pitched their plot ideas to Tony, the only person who really counted in the room, who could at will erase any scene or character he did not fully approve of and replace it without opposition with an invention of his own. Suddenly Matthew realized uneasily that some of the eeriness he had been lately experiencing derived from the extraordinary power that Tony unquestionably had and was exercising over their lives: no matter what he did, they dreaded even contradicting, let alone standing up to him.

Throughout the long evening, Tony had been sipping slowly but steadily from a nearby cup, attentively replenished by Emma or Betty, who seemed to compete for the honor. Now he stood up, yawned mightily, and boorishly stretched out his arms. It was an unsubtle signal and permission for the group to disperse. Announcing that she was quite tired and would be going to bed, Emma excused herself from the table, and only then—with Emma safely removed—did Betty follow suit. Noting that he had an upcoming TV commercial, his first since arriving in Los Angeles, and therefore needed all the rest he could get, Bobby made his way out the rear door, which led directly to the backyard of his own house. Then Jay, who had been especially taciturn and had looked plain scared throughout the entire meeting, got up from his chair, mumbled "good-night," and, after looking suspiciously around the room, as though to verify that no one was going to stop him, edged out of the living room and up the staircase toward his own bedroom, which was adjacent to Emma's on the second floor.

It seemed the perfect time for Matthew, who, like the others, felt drained and exhausted from the tension of the meeting, to make his exit, and trying to appear as nonchalant as possible, he began to get up from his chair, but Tony stopped him. "Don't go. I have something to show you."

Matthew instantly complied, inadvertently catching the eye of Sean, the forgotten man in the room, who was sitting so quietly that he might have been praying. Good. At least he was not alone in the room with Tony, who now, he could no longer deny, was beginning to terrify him and who, satisfied that Matthew was staying, crossed over to the mantel of the unused fireplace.

Finding what he was looking for—a short-handled iron ax, one of the weapons he occasionally collected and that he proudly claimed to be an early American original—he laid it slowly in the center of the table beside the now-empty gallon of Chablis wine.

After a long dramatic pause, during which he stared pensively first at one and then the other, Tony inquired, "Have you seen this?"

Too frightened to think on his feet, Matthew could only respond literally, "I've seen it several times in the house."

"I mean, didn't you see Jay bring it down tonight?"

Matthew could not recall how the ax came to be put upon the mantel, but he was quite sure that when Jay had entered the room for the eight o'clock meeting he had not been carrying it, and he softly answered, "I didn't see Jay with an ax tonight."

"Oh, no? Then look at this." Returning to the mantel, Tony retrieved the sheet of white paper he had placed there, as evidence, early in the day and kept for just this occasion, and with a triumphant sneer handed it to Matthew.

On it was a very grim caricature of Tony, done in bold black ink; and the fact that its subject was so clearly recognizable betrayed its authorship by Jay, who was a talented cartoonist as well as a playwright.

Relieved that the tenor of another eerie conversation was perhaps shifting to something as safely banal as a caricature, Matthew, feigning enthusiasm, volunteered, "It looks like you."

"Yes, it does. But what would you say the man who drew this thinks about the subject? What is he trying to say?"

"Well, he looks stern, tough."

"He looks evil. This is the picture of an evil satyr."

Now that it had been pointed out, the man in the picture did look somewhat evil, but Matthew for some reason was afraid to admit it. "He does look kind of cruel. So?"

Tony picked up the caricature in one hand and the ax in the other.

"Don't you get it yet? It was an assassination attempt. Jay came down here with the ax tonight in order to murder me. But when he saw how much the Frontiersmen love me, he didn't have the guts to go through with it.

"Ever since I announced that the New York Frontiersmen would be arriving tomorrow, I could smell an assassination attempt, I had a sixth sense, but I didn't think it would come from someone in my own house. When Jay showed me the picture this morning, I knew he was the one. And when I saw the ax on the mantel when I came into the living room tonight, I knew that Jay had taken it from my bedroom in order to murder me."

It was past midnight. The rear door had been left ajar by Bobby when he had left, and a chill breeze was blowing through the room. Tony continued to sit shirtless, but now tears were running from his eyes.

"I'm a good man, you know. I have a bad temper, and I was always afraid that I would kill someone someday, but I am a good man. Jay thinks I'm evil, and wants to kill me before I unite the Frontiersmen tomorrow.

"I'm a good man, but I can't let Jay do that. Tomorrow, after they come, in front of the Frontiersmen, I'm going to cave Jay's head in with this."

Tony shook the ax in his fist, as though to punctuate his threat, replaced it on the table, then looked somberly at Matthew and Sean, waiting for a reaction and an affirmation.

Matthew did not have to glance over at Sean to know that he was sitting transfixed in his chair. His own fear he would characterize as a heart-stopping quiet dread, which would neither fully paralyze him nor impel him toward the self-protective path of defense or escape. Instead, he would be what he could always be, especially in a crisis—a survivor—and to sustain himself against the unbearable tension, he would draw upon what he considered his greatest strength, his loyalty. His loyalty to his leader, however dangerously irrational he now appeared, and his loyalty to his friend, Jay, who seemed on the brink of being maimed or killed (although he could not bring himself to believe that).

There did not seem time to question whether Tony was sane or insane, to examine his own proximity to possible mortal danger, to exercise "reality testing." It was necessary, in order to survive, that he suspend the conventional mode of responding to the practical world (not that he had ever been much good at that), and instead immerse himself in and keep step with the rhythm of the chaos that was his present reality and seemed to be engulfing him, as one in a dream state embraces, and then tries to adjust to, the impossible logic of a nightmare.

And because of his extreme loyalty, it would not be enough for Matthew merely to survive. Jay, who seemed on the verge of being violently assaulted, must also survive, and especially Tony, who, against all reason, was publicly perpetrating a murder. So, stifling his panic, using the nobility of his intentions to rally himself, Matthew called upon one other outstanding talent: his ability to read people's needs like a book, to have an uncanny grasp of whatever was necessary to calm someone down.

So, banking on the fact that he knew Tony perhaps better than anyone else in the world, and taking his courage in his hands, he dared to disagree, gently pointing out that he was certain he had seen Jay enter the living room minus the ax; admitting that while the caricature did seem to exude an evil persona, it did not follow that Jay necessarily considered him an evil man, and that even if he did, it still did not follow, given Jay's passive personality, that he could ever be capable of such a viciously cold-blooded crime; and in turn pretending to deliberate upon whatever Tony said, before patiently returning to the defense of his friend.

His mistake was to use logic where logic could not prevail, to try to make sense of what was senseless, and when it dawned on Matthew that even his most eloquent rhetoric had no power to make Tony swerve one jot from the intended pathway of his brutal thought, and fearing that he had already gone too far, he stopped. But it was too late. Tony's face was beginning to transform, his cheeks seeming to fill up with blood, the veins protruding from his temples, his eyes twitching. Never had Matthew seen such visceral hatred in a human face. Never had he heard such a hideous bellow:

"YOOOOOUUU COCKSUCKER!
YOU'RE ON HIS SIDE. GET OUT!"

His courage deserting him, Matthew stumbled against his chair as he leaped to his feet, continued to stumble as he lurched toward the rear door, which thankfully was still ajar, and as he made his escape, as though it were diabolically pursuing him,

Matthew heard the wine jug shatter as it struck the door behind him. Once outside the house, he started to run, and although he kept losing his footing and falling, he kept on running until he reached the comparative safety of his own backyard.

The distance separating the two backyards was not more than fifty yards, but Matthew could not have been more winded had he been running a mile. Supporting himself on the porch railing, as he gasped for air, he felt his courage return, and with it a sense of defiance that was new. "You devil, you won't get me." He spoke the words aloud to no one in particular, alone in the cold, cloudless, starry night. Fifty yards away, over the broken fence meant to divide the two backyards, through the swaying branches of a single overhanging tree, the lights from the living room of Tony's house were still shining in the glass pane of the rear door. Outrageous, obnoxious, impossible, incredibly arrogant, wildly original, yes—but essentially a good man: that is how Matthew had thought of his friend. Tonight that picture had changed forever, and he allowed himself to dare to wonder, for the very first time, if his friend might actually be evil, and even, as the hideous unreality and trauma of what had transpired began to sink in ... perhaps not human. Feeling banished from his one sanctuary in the world, the Cult, Matthew felt dangerously and helplessly isolated, and scarcely in a position to offer opposition. He had recovered his breath, but his heart was beating fiercely. What if Tony left the house and came after him? What would he do?

There were things he would not do, because he was not capable, not then, of even thinking of them. He would not call the police. He would not run. He would not leave, not dare to think of voluntarily quitting the Cult of the Frontiersmen. What he would do was stand his ground, fatalistically wait to see what was in store for him, and passionately defend himself should Tony persist in accusing him of somehow being involved in an assassination attempt upon his life. Although he was terrified of the possibility, he refused to believe that Tony could actually come after him with the ax, but he also knew that should Tony do so, he would not be able to defend himself physically, and it was this

retrospective realization—that because of his symbiotic identification with the leader and the cult, he actually believed that Tony,
evil or not, had more of a right to take his life than he had to
defend it—that contributed more than anything else to his
shameful sense of having been toyed with.

After some moments of such literally existential thinking, and
relieved that nothing had happened, Matthew opened the back
door of his own house and walked into his own living room. He
did not know which frightened him more, the stillness of the
house, reinforcing his sense of solitude, or the echo of his footsteps on the wooden floor, signaling his whereabouts. Better to
take off his shoes. By now he was used to his accelerated heart-
beat and would no longer mind it for the remainder of the night.
On an impulse, he walked into the kitchen, opened the cabinet
where Bobby kept a carton of Lucky Strike cigarettes, and
removed a fresh pack. It had been three years since he had
stopped smoking, after his coughing fits had warned him that
nicotine and bronchitis did not go together, but he had recently
been dreaming about smoking, and now seemed a perfect time
to resume. He opened the pack, slid a cigarette out, lit it at the
gas range, and, carrying his shoes in one hand, padded up two
flights of stairs. He paused outside the closed door of Bobby's
bedroom, which was down the hall from his own, and listened to
his faint snoring. He was not disappointed, perhaps even
relieved. Bursting as he was to tell someone what had happened,
he could not help dreading the aftermath of such a disclosure.

There was no one in the cult, other than Tony, whom Matthew
liked more, and he believed that Bobby felt the same way about
him, but he was not stupid. Bobby, like everyone else, including
himself, had only one unshakable allegiance, and that was to
Tony. Great as his affection may have been for Matthew, there was
not the slightest doubt that should a conflict of loyalties arise,
Bobby would throw in his lot with Tony.

And (since he could not trust him) feeling that it was better
for both of them if Bobby continued to rest up for his TV commercial, Matthew headed down the hall to what seemed the only

place in the house where he could safely go—his own bedroom. He did not lock the door—that would be pointless. Whether that night, the next morning, or the next day, sooner or later Tony would come for him. He was certain of that. His dilemma, as he saw it, was not when but how. Exactly what would Tony say to him, accuse him of, and how best should he counter? That was the crux. Trying to still his racing emotions, Matthew forced himself to relive the events of the night and place them in the context of his long history with Tony, desperately searching for a key to resolve, in a benign way, a hellish puzzle.

He sat in the dark by his bedroom window, where he had a clear view of the rear of Tony's house, still lighted, and smoked one cigarette after another. The slightest noise startled him, and until he could assure himself that he had not heard footsteps, he panicked. After five such peaceful hours of keeping watch by his bedroom window, he became embarrassed, then angry, with himself for being so skittish. He scolded himself for thinking during the long sleepless night only of himself and not once about Jay, the person who was perhaps really in danger, and he devoted himself for at least an hour to a risky consideration of how he might still rescue his friend.

In the early morning light and with the singing of the birds, it became quite clear to Matthew that the way to save Jay would not be through Tony: not through an appeal to reason, nor an entreaty for mercy. It would have to be through Jay—Matthew would have to tell him, face to face, what had happened and warn him of what was about to happen. But how? And when? The lights had been turned out hours ago, and from his bedroom aerie Tony's house looked asleep; but he could not be sure, and he knew he would never find the courage to steal up to Jay's bedroom and surreptitiously signal him. That meant somehow contriving to catch Jay alone, perhaps after Tony had driven to the airport to pick up the incoming disciples—which he would not fail to do—warning him as quickly and effectively as he could, all the while taking care that no one who might inform, which included everyone, should see him.

So that was that. It felt like heart-pounding high adventure, and once he had decided to do it he felt better about himself than he had for a very long time. It was six o'clock in the morning. Matthew ground out his remaining Lucky Strike and wondered if it were desirable, or possible, for him to sleep a little.

Without warning, a downstairs door banged open, followed by unmistakable footsteps and the even more unmistakable voice of Tony ringing through the house.

"Matthew ... Matthew ... Come on down."

So cheery and normal did it sound, so much the voice he had been waiting to hear, that Matthew, without fear, instinctively left the sanctuary of his bedroom and approached the head of the stairs.

Fully dressed now, and inexplicably ebullient, Tony beckoned him from below. "Come on down. Don't be afraid."

Relieved that it was over, but beginning to feel angry that he had been unnecessarily and unfairly put through the wringer (and hoping at least for an apology, if not an explanation), Matthew went downstairs and sullenly stood by the side of his mentor, who exuberantly threw his arm around his shoulders.

"Buddy, it's going to be a great day. We're meeting the New York Frontiersmen at the airport at five o'clock. Hey! What happened to you?"

Like a solicitous parent, Tony moved to within inches of Matthew's face in order to inspect crimson splotches appearing on his forehead and cheeks: burst blood vessels, which Matthew sometimes incurred as a result of excessive alcohol, which he had already seen in the bathroom mirror, and which he now saw as an opportunity to instill guilt in his friend.

"I had a rough night, you know."

Tony could not have looked more confused. "What are you talking about?"

"You threw me out of the house. I had nothing to do with Jay, and besides, I don't believe Jay had any intention of hurting you."

Indignant, as though his authority and judgment were being falsely called into question, Tony became assertively stern. "Make no mistake about it, Matthew. It was an assassination attempt, all right. I'm not saying you were in on it—but you did take his side."

Inwardly fuming and feeling secure enough to argue, Matthew shot back, "I took his side because I thought he was innocent."

"You took his side because you were afraid to face the truth. Do you know who you reminded me of last night?"

"Who?"

In a fatherly way, Tony rested his hand on Matthew's shoulder.

"Judas. You should have seen your face. I have never seen such pain and suffering before. The guilt in your face over having betrayed me, just before you ran out the door, was actually beautiful. It was the face of Judas in the painting of the *Last Supper*."

Matthew looked down, hopeless at the realization that the bond that had always existed between him and Tony had somehow been destroyed, and that they would never again be able to understand and speak to one another in the old way. He thought of the thirty pieces of silver that had once been mailed to Michael, and his premonition that one day he might be placed in the same category. When Tony once more invited him to meet the Frontiersmen at the airport, he excused himself on the grounds of illness, and when he was told that everyone else—except Betty, who tended to be phobic and rarely left the house, and Jay, who was known to become carsick—would be going, he recognized that fate was presenting him with a golden opportunity.

During the remainder of the morning and the early afternoon Matthew plotted how best to break the news to Jay. How do you warn a person that you have definite knowledge that someone may be planning to murder him? Is there a tactful way to do it? His instinct was to soft-pedal the violence and relay the information in as hopeful and reassuring a light as possible, but he was objective enough to apprehend that candor and not tact would be most beneficial to Jay.

He watched as Tony boisterously directed the disciples to two cars, which, on his signal to proceed, headed down the avenue in the direction of the airport. He had made sure to count each disciple in each of the cars, so as to confirm that besides himself only Betty and Jay had been left behind. He noted that Betty, after enthusiastically waving good-bye from her front porch, immediately went back into the house. And only then did he cautiously circle his own house to mislead anyone who might be snooping, make his way through the dilapidated fence supposedly dividing the contiguous backyards, and let himself in through the rear door, which was generally open, of Tony's house.

Judging from Tony's behavior of this morning, Matthew no longer believed that he was intent upon exacting vengeance upon Jay, but so fantastic had been his mood swings of late, that he could not speak for this evening. Better to warn Jay; and if he were going to do it, he had to do it quickly because he knew he was much too frightened to prolong it. As was Jay: the group "neurotic," the most high-strung, easily intimidated, and therefore most picked-on of all.

Matthew found him sitting in an armchair pulled alongside the unused fireplace. As usual, he was reading a book. Drawing up a chair of his own, and positioning himself at an angle to the large facing window, Matthew tried, given the circumstances, to appear fairly but not falsely calm. He began by softly saying he had something to tell him.

Jay put down the book, instantly alarmed.

"What?"

"It's about last night. Something that happened between me and Tony after you left."

"Does it concern me?"

"Yes."

"What is it?"

"First you must swear ... you must swear not to tell anyone, especially Tony, what I tell you. Do you swear?"

His blue eyes wide with terror at the injunction to secrecy—which he was well aware would infuriate Tony should he learn of it—Jay feebly protested, "Why do I have to swear?"

"You have to, or I won't tell you."

"I swear."

Matthew laid his hand gently on Jay's shoulder. Of the count-
less ways to break the news, he had decided brevity and honesty
were the best, and to achieve that he had simply to fall back upon
his excellent, near-total recall and repeat verbatim the exchange
between Tony and himself concerning Jay, as soon as he had said
good-night and left the room. But first he made a point of prefac-
ing his bombshell by emphasizing the vastly improved frame of
mind that Tony had appeared to be in all morning, and he reaf-
firmed, several times, "I told Tony I did not believe this ... and I
want you to know I stuck up for you."

Then he described what had happened as quickly and objectively as he could.

Jay turned white. "Are you kidding? It was just a picture!"

"Tony wasn't kidding, believe me."

"But he wasn't upset when I showed it to him. He even
laughed over it."

"I couldn't figure it out either, Jay. He's under so much pressure these days ... he's acting weird."

"Oh, my God. What should I do?"

What surprised Matthew was not that Jay looked ready to collapse in tears, but that he had made such a heartfelt appeal for
his friend to save him. Never had Matthew felt so trusted. Never
had the loyalty he prided himself on, his ability to stand by someone in a crisis, been so called upon. More inspired than ever to
rescue his friend, his thinking became correspondingly bolder,
and he remembered the bicycle Jay kept in his room (as a hedge
against being forced to rely upon rides in cars) and his penchant
for traveling with a backpack.

In a display of fatherly strength that secretly thrilled him,
Matthew responded to Jay's plea for guidance. "I think you
should go."

"I should go?"

It took a few moments, but as soon as it had sunk in, this made
perfect sense to Jay, who nodded and ran up the steps to his
room. Within fifteen minutes he had returned, all the belongings

in the world that he cared about on his back, and his means of escape in his hands. As he watched him bicycle up the street, Matthew felt a brief flurry of panic over what Tony might do to him should he ever find out, but he told himself that Tony would not find out, and forced himself instead to concentrate on Jay and everything they had been through together as friends during the past two years, suspecting that he would never see him again.

That was the marker, the episode he referred to as the "first big trauma." Matthew realized upon returning to his own house to await the arrival of the reunited Frontiersmen from the airport that things would never be the same—not only between Tony and himself, but between Tony and everyone else—if only because Tony's confidence and sense of power would grow in leaps and bounds in proportion to the number of Frontiersmen surrounding him, and off whom he fed.

The change was apparent even in the twin parties, one in Betty's house and one in Emma's, that Tony hastily arranged in order to celebrate the arrival, at last, of the New York Frontiersmen. For one thing, over and above the usual merriment, boasting, and competitive put-downs that were a staple of such occasions, Tony was now talking and shouting at an abnormally fast, nonstop pace, spewing forth strategy upon strategy, making glorious predictions about what lay in store for the Frontiersmen, and above all, dispatching orders.

It was strange at first how docile and malleable the New York Frontiersmen seemed to whatever Tony proposed, until it dawned on Matthew that they had been pre-indoctrinated and perhaps already traumatized by the secret meeting that Tony had called in the Statler Hilton Hotel, and amazingly had superintended, step by step, over the long-distance telephone. Matthew could find no other explanation for the cowed, feckless way in which the muscular Stuart, who had once gunned down a charging black bear; the meticulously logical Ted; the passionate, power-loving Julian; the self-proclaimed rebel Glen; and the comically free-spirited Cliff immediately and unanimously assented to even the most preposterous-sounding ideas put forward by Tony.

If such submission could be induced solely by long-distance telephone, Matthew did not want to estimate how much more Tony could elicit in person, especially with his new demonically supercharged personality. Instead, he thought about how best to pretend to be at ease so as to deflect unwanted attention from himself. He had never before opposed Tony as he had by clandestinely revealing to Jay what he had said, and he was certain that should Tony hear of it, or worse, figure it out in that ingenious way of his, then conceivably he, Matthew, could be regarded as the greatest traitor of all, greater even than Michael or Jay. He must not, therefore, show how frightened he was feeling, because that would be a giveaway. He must not shrink within himself, give in to his impulse to hide from the eyes of others, or become apprehensive over the fact that not once during the festivities had Tony exchanged a friendly glance—because that too would be a giveaway.

So Matthew bit his lip, and waited. Amazingly, not once in the course of a long night of drinking and desperate reveling had anyone mentioned Jay's name, or commented on his unexplained absence. It was now past midnight, and the party had traveled from Betty's house back to Emma's, when out of the blue, Sean announced, "I think Jay has taken off."

Tony seemed genuinely perplexed. "What do you mean?"

"Well, the door to his room is wide open, and his bicycle and all his belongings are gone."

At first Tony considered this a psychological mystery, to be understood only by unraveling the inner workings of Jay's mind. Only when this line of reasoning led nowhere did he see the connection between Jay's disappearance and his own threat, just twenty-four hours ago, to murder him.

Rising from his chair, positioned once again at the head of the massive black table, Tony strode over to the fireplace mantel and dramatically retrieved the ax, which he had apparently replaced after Matthew had fled. Returning to his chair and setting the ax carefully back on the table, Tony turned to the assembled Frontiersmen with an almost mystical fervor.

"Last night there was an assassination attempt against my life and tonight there was going to be a pay back execution. But that clever bastard must have figured it out."

A strange hush descended on the room as Tony chronicled the events of the previous night as viewed from his own unwavering persecutory perspective. When he arrived at the point where he had accused Matthew, he sneeringly added, "Judas over there was too cowardly to face the truth. He actually defended Jay."

For a moment Matthew, no longer afraid, felt as if it might be better to die rather than continue to bear this. He saw, however, that he was not about to die, that Tony's deliberately sardonic public reference to him as "Judas" was meant to put him in his place, and was all the punishment he would receive—at least until the next mood change. Realizing this, and seeing that it would continue, he renewed his resolve to survive somehow: and although he may have helped save Jay, he knew he did not have the strength or the courage to repeat what he had done with any of the others. Perhaps utilizing his talent for calming Tony down, in spite of their present rift, might actually make matters less dangerous for everyone concerned; perhaps not. All he could really concentrate on was personally surviving.

And because it never occurred to Matthew that survival was possible, even necessary, outside of the cult and away from the aegis of Tony, he automatically stayed.

Making up for the previous night by sleeping more soundly then he had for a long time, Matthew awoke in the afternoon of the following day, to the change of lifestyle he had anticipated and feared. Already, at Tony's request, Julian and Ted had not only moved all their belongings into his downstairs living room but had been sent off on some mission, while Stuart, Glen, and Cliff had been allocated to Betty's and Emma's. Matthew took a walk around the block to get his bearings. When he came to the sidewalk directly in front of Betty's house, he accelerated his pace so as not to be spotted, but he could not resist a nervous, sideways, spying glance. It was just as well that he saw nothing and no one through the front door, which curiously had been flung open. Relieved, but thinking it odd that he had not yet been seen, he continued circling the block until he arrived at the front porch of Emma's.

Sitting on the steps was Sean, who obviously was happy to see his friend. He looked awful to Matthew, almost as frightened as when he had sat transfixed in his chair, an image that would always stay with him. Something must have happened, but Matthew was afraid to ask, increasingly fearful that whatever he said and did might somehow get reported back to Tony.

Sean must have felt the same, because before saying what he wanted to say, he approached to within a foot of Matthew's ear. And although no one was within fifty feet of either of them, in a whisper he inquired, "Do you know what happened at the meeting at Betty's house this morning?"

"I was sleeping."

"Sleeping?"

"Yes. After Tony threw me out of the house the other night, I didn't sleep much."

"Oh. Well, you weren't missed. Tony was so busy telling people what had to be done. It was kind of incredible. Stuart, Glen, and Cliff have been ordered to produce an acceptable outline for a screenplay within five days, and they're going nuts in their rooms trying to do it. Ted and Julian have already left in a car for Las Vegas."

"Las Vegas?"

"They have to contact a Texas oil billionaire, Joe Luire, who is supposed to be down there, and persuade him to loan money to the Frontiersmen."

"How are they going to do that?"

Sean laughed sheepishly. "Tony has a plan, but it's another secret." Then, moving a few inches nearer to Matthew's ear, he asked, "Do you want to hear something weird that happened to me this morning?"

Matthew nodded and edged even closer to Sean, who was becoming progressively less audible.

"This morning, around seven o'clock, I was sitting in my bedroom, thinking. I heard this noise in my closet, you know the one with sliding doors. At first it sounded like a rustling, like the clothes were moving. Then there was a scratching noise. I thought maybe it was a rat. I think I was hoping it was a rat. But a few seconds later through the opening in the doors I saw something begin to move from behind the clothes.

"Suddenly Tony appeared. He had been hiding in the closet. I don't know how he got in there or how long he had been hiding. Maybe when I went to the bathroom, but that was an hour ago. It scared the shit out of me. He stepped out of the closet, said, 'Excuse me,' with a sarcastic smile, and walked out of the room."

Sean looked quickly behind his back to make doubly sure no one was within hearing, before plaintively whispering, "Matthew, do you know what's going to happen?"

"I think Tony's under a lot of pressure ever since he decided to bring everybody out to California. It'll be all right, though." As soon as he said it, it sounded phony and scarcely comforting, as he had intended, and Matthew realized that in spite of his own rising bitterness and skepticism, his loyalty remained unchanged, and at the first hint of a breach of faith in their leader, he was compelled to defend Tony.

Grateful that no one besides Sean had seen him, Matthew retraced his steps. He had forgotten to ask Sean whether Tony had given him an assignment, as he had the others, and he began to wonder if the fact that so far nothing had been delegated to him was a portent of the shrinking significance he was acquiring in the mind of Tony.

Suddenly Matthew, who was approaching Betty's house from the opposite direction, and thus had a direct view into the living room through a side window, stopped short, frozen at the sight of a man tilted backward in an armchair, his body wrapped in an enormous sheet, his hair being cut by a man he had never seen before, who was holding a scissors in his right hand. Despite the uncanny impression it made on him, Matthew recognized that the man in the armchair, who seemed to be staring majestically at the ceiling, was Tony, and the stranger behind him in a white coat was a professional barber, no doubt from a local barbershop. Intuitively Matthew understood the meaning of the symbol: Tony, who had always professed to love the kings of old and their power, was by this act proclaiming himself to be, at last, a king on earth.

For about a minute he stood and watched the man who would be king, his king, having his hair cut, and savoring it like a forbidden pleasure. It was a display of avidity that both fascinated and disgusted him. Shuddering, he hid his face so as not to be seen, rushed into his own house, and closeted himself once more within the sanctuary of his bedroom. Matthew spent the remainder of the afternoon and the evening chain-smoking and periodically sipping from a cup that he kept filled with Chablis.

He refused to consider whether it was a good or a bad sign that no one had come for him and no one had requested his company. Instead, he concentrated on getting drunk, and the drunker he became the more he congratulated himself on perhaps having discovered what he had been looking for: a relatively painless and speedy way of surviving. Although he generally suffered from severe hangovers when he drank to excess, as well as occasional burst blood vessels, he not only would incur no ill effects but would, uncharacteristically, thoroughly enjoy his night of solitary revelry; and that was because on some level he realized that it would be his last, and that in the days to come his time would no longer be his own.

The rapping on his door came at six in the morning, cutting short what promised to be a second night of uninterrupted sleep. The good news was that it was Bobby. The bad news was that Tony was already waiting for him downstairs, apparently annoyed that he had missed yesterday's meeting at Betty's.

Quickly Matthew slipped on a T-shirt and a pair of Bermuda shorts and grimly headed for the staircase. It had been days since he last shaved, and his new scruffy look matched his mood: tougher, number, and more cynically antisocial.

He was surprised to find Tony seated on the couch, not only fully dressed but dressed in his best dark blue suit, with a pressed

shirt and sporting his favorite maroon tie. While he looked as if
he were about to set out on the first day of a new job, Matthew
knew Tony had not worked since arriving in California, and he
wondered if this get-up were somehow connected to yesterday's
private barber, and were another symbol heralding the inauguration of a royal identity.

Matthew pulled up a chair and waited grumpily. He noted that
Tony had descended from his ebullience and was now the picture
of sobriety.

"You know my theory, don't you, about who really killed
Kennedy?"

Wearily, Matthew nodded. About a dozen times, since shortly
after they had arrived in Los Angeles he had been buttonholed
by Tony and forced to act as a sounding board for the latest spin
on his evolving theory of who really killed John F. Kennedy, and
why. Eventually it came down to a Machiavellian conspiracy mas-
terminded by an envious, Cassius-like Lyndon Baines Johnson,
executed by the clandestine CIA, and backed up by a support
team from the mob—and while such talk never failed to unnerve
Matthew and turn him off, he had always felt it was his obligation
at least to pretend to listen. Now he saw that much more than
that was going to be required of him.

"Good. Because now we're going to cash in on it."

"Cash in?"

"The Frontiersmen are running short of cash, and I've
decided to squeeze Frank."

"Frank who?"

Tony smiled in anticipation of how what he was about to say
would be sure to spook Matthew. "Sinatra."

"Frank Sinatra!"

He turned pale at the hideous thing he sensed Tony was going
to try to force him to do, simultaneously realizing that what he
was about to hear would constitute his assignment.

"You know about Sinatra's underworld connections. He therefore had to know about the mob's involvement in the CIA's conspiracy to murder Kennedy, but of course he has to cover it up.

This is what I want you to do. Call up Frank Sinatra personally, get him on the telephone, I don't care how you do it, and say, say exactly this: 'Mr. Sinatra, Tony West is investigating the murder of John F. Kennedy and thinks it would be better if you financed our efforts.' Say that, he'll know what it means."

Matthew could feel his heart pounding, but could offer only token resistance. "That's extortion!"

Suddenly Tony, with an irritable look, reached over and with the heel of his right hand rammed Matthew in the forehead, hard enough to make him blink. "*Really*? Just do it. Start at nine in the morning on the telephone. Bobby will be helping you on the other phone, and remember, don't get off until you've gotten at least a fifty-thousand check. I'll be keeping my eye on you, so don't goof off."

Even more upsetting than the impossibility of such an arrangement was Tony's absolute, almost mystical certainty that it not only could but *would* be carried out to his complete satisfaction. Matthew felt helpless. On the one hand, he could not count on Bobby, his best friend, because whenever Bobby was scared, as he had to be now, he became righteous and rigid, which meant he would be terrified of departing one iota from Tony's instructions, regardless of how insane they sounded. On the other hand, to *dare* openly refuse to follow out the instructions might be tantamount in Tony's mind to confirmation that Matthew was, as he supposed, a real Judas.

While that would be dangerous, Matthew also knew that it was impossible, even if his very life depended upon it, to extort money from anyone. Certainly not from Frank Sinatra, who was one of his heroes, and whom, ironically, he had always loyally and persistently defended against allegations of underworld affiliations. It meant that he therefore could not carry out Tony's instructions, which in turn meant that he was putting himself in the unhealthy position of being regarded as a Judas. In a flash the way out came to Matthew: he must go through the motions of doing what Tony wanted without really doing it, yet without letting Tony know that he was secretly sabotaging his orders.

During the next several hours, up until the designated starting time of nine A.M., Matthew tried to concoct a telephone sales pitch that would seem to a casual eavesdropper to be a bona-fide extortion attempt, but would in actuality be only a clever counterfeit. To do that, he would have to make subtle but important changes in Tony's message. The first change was to substitute "would you consider" for the more sinister "it would be better." The second change was the addition of an innocuous but necessary "it would be appreciated." And the third change was to him the most subtle, crucial, and ingenious of all: by simply using his beautifully modulated, soothing voice, Matthew—regardless of whatever words were forced out of him—would be able to deliver the nonverbal message that there was absolutely nothing to be frightened of.

At nine A.M., confident that he had come up with the best plan possible, Matthew picked up the telephone in his bedroom and started dialing, as did Bobby in his room down the hall. Although he knew it would not be easy, he was about to discover how truly unreachable Frank Sinatra really was: after two hours of continuous dialing, after leaving numerous telephone messages on dozens of answering machines, he had nothing to show for it.

By twelve noon, Matthew had yet to make contact with a single non-recorded voice that had anything remotely to do with Frank Sinatra. By one, he was beginning to fear that unless he could produce a series of near-misses or at least respectable attempts, then he could easily be accused of not genuinely trying; and again, in Tony's mind, that could be equivalent to a betrayal. By two, when he had still not reached anyone live, he was sweating and had to fight off an incipient wave of panic. In spite of himself, he kept anxiously scanning the room to reassure himself that Tony had not somehow slipped in and hidden himself in the closet, or perhaps under the bed, so as to trap him. Or, in Matthew's fantasy, to appear suddenly and point menacingly at his watch to signify his rage at Matthew's failure to execute his orders. And in a sense, it was Tony's genius for bullying and terrorizing that he did not do this, that instinctively he pounced only when least expected to.

But because he was so preoccupied defending himself against accusations that never came, Matthew nearly jumped out of his chair when at two forty-five the telephone at last rang.

"Is this Matthew, of Tony West Enterprises?"

"Yes."

"This is Patricia Denby of Mr. Sinatra's office."

"Mr. West is investigating the murder of John F. Kennedy. He would appreciate it if it would be possible for Mr. Sinatra to contribute a loan?"

"Excuse me?"

"Mr. West needs funds to continue the investigation."

"What does that have to do with Mr. Sinatra?"

"Mr. West is seeking the help of prominent people in the entertainment industry who are concerned citizens to help with this important investigation."

"I still don't see a connection with Mr. Sinatra."

"Miss Denby, could you please just deliver the message to Mr. Sinatra? It's *very, very* urgent. It would mean a lot to Mr. West, really."

"I'll deliver the message."

Although Matthew's hands were shaking, he felt he had done what he wanted to do. He now had something to show for his marathon telephoning, something to tell Tony about. During his sole telephone conversation, he had briefly panicked when he had felt his predetermined calm suddenly giving way to a strident (to his own ears) tone of coercive pleading. Had he been so cowed by the pressure of the moment that he had been seduced, in spite of himself, into coming across as an extortionist in order to achieve his aim? He had brushed the thought aside, regained his cool, and managed to convince Patricia Denby to relay Tony West's request for a loan.

It was enough to drain the tension from his body and wash away the terror from his brain. He did not even notice when five o'clock, the cut-off time, rolled around, and would not have noticed had not Bobby, who looked exhausted, agitated, and worried sick, entered the room.

"I didn't get a single loan."

Matthew could see that Bobby, in his frightened, rigid way, was relying too heavily on the letter of the law—but before he could say that to him, the lawmaker appeared, standing a few feet behind Bobby. Eleven hours had passed, but he was dressed no less impeccably then he had been at six in the morning. Absent from his face was any hoped-for trace of insouciance; instead, it bore a grim expression of restrained but deadly seriousness.

Looking sharply at both Matthew and Bobby, he tapped the face of his watch, exactly as Matthew had fantasized, in a brisk way that somehow managed to convey a world of menace.

"Well?"

Bobby made the mistake of being too honest, of reporting letter-of-the-law failures, instead of partial, well-intended, and perhaps thereby calming successes, and he simply reiterated, "I didn't get a single loan."

Without warning, Tony furiously struck Bobby on the side of his head with the heel of his right hand, a considerably harder blow than the one delivered this morning to Matthew and the force of which sent Bobby reeling backward.

"But Tony, I was calling all day."

As Tony stepped forward, evidently to continue the assault, Matthew, feigning enthusiasm, tried to intercede. "I spoke to a Patricia Denby, who promised to relay your message to Frank Sinatra."

At that instant the telephone rang, for only the second time, and Tony, still in a rage, lunged for it.

"Yes?"

The voice on the other end, rough and cocky, identified itself as "Mr. Marble of Frank Sinatra's office" and asked to speak to Mr. Tony West.

Glancing at his watch, and winking broadly at both of them, Tony arrogantly cut Mr. Marble short with a ridiculous rebuke. "You're calling past business hours."

"So?" responded the voice in a matching wise-guy tone.

"So what do you want?"

"I understand that a Mr. Tony West has been asking for money from Mr. Sinatra. Is that correct?"

"Absolutely not. You see, there's been an imposter running around town who's saying he's me."

"You're Tony West?"

"Yes."

"I am to understand then that you are *not* asking for any money from Mr. Sinatra?"

"Absolutely not!"

To Matthew—given that in Tony's mind, as he would later insist, he had toyed with and openly mocked a man he considered a dangerous mafioso—it was an example of stunning fearlessness, and lost in admiration, he was able momentarily to put aside his fuming anger that his leader had apparently developed a new trait: beating disciples whom he considered disobedient as though they were dogs.

What Matthew did not see, and was not ready to see, was that in spite of his outrageous bluff, Tony upon realizing that his intimidation was not going to work with Mr. Marble, had backed down.

He began counting the days, comparing and remembering them according to their dramatic content. Day One was the first big trauma, when Tony announced his intention to execute the disciple who was planning to assassinate him, and then branded Matthew a Judas for siding with the assassin. Day Two was Matthew's great act of bravado, when he may have saved Jay's life by warning him what Tony was planning to do. Day Three was the moratorium, when Matthew got pleasantly drunk, but it was noteworthy for the eerie spectacle of Tony being royally attended to by a personal barber. And Day Four was the disgusting attempt to extort money from Frank Sinatra.

For Matthew, Day One would always be *the day*, against which all other days would be assessed for their intensity, but for everyone else Days Five and Six, together, would be the paradigmatic horror. It began in a comparatively low-key manner, at eight in the

62

morning, with Tony, as always, at the hub of a group of people assembled in the back porch of Emma's house. (Later, in a genuine leap of insight, Matthew would connect the two paradigmatic days of horror, both of which would occur at Emma's house, to his remembrance of Tony sobbing over her threat not to join him in California—and would understand that it was the dynamics of Tony's relationship to Emma, more than to anyone else, that seemed to precipitate his wildest flights of irrationality.)

Together they seemed to be intently investigating something, and when Matthew approached, Tony, grasping his shoulder in a friendly way and leading him to the object of their inquiry, invited him to participate.

"Hey, Matthew, look at this."

What they were looking at was the outer door frame, specifically at a telephone wire that ran alongside it before disappearing through a hole into the house. With his forefinger, Tony trailed the wire for a critical yard, carefully pointing to a series of damning discrepancies: here the wire was painted black, there it was gray, here was white plaster molding firmly in place, there just six inches away was white plaster molding mysteriously beginning to rot.

He had risen at six in the morning, as he had every day during the past week, to patrol the block in order to safeguard the three houses containing his precious but vulnerable Frontiersmen, and a sixth sense had directed him to the tampering. He had suspected for a long while that ever since Emma had arrived he had been under surveillance, but he had never imagined or even dreamed of the possibility that his telephone might actually be tapped.

Satisfied that he had more than evidence, he had proof, Tony waved everyone into the living room, where they convened around the ritual black dining table and were enjoined, like a jury, to pass judgment on the physical evidence that had been presented and vote on the grave allegation of wiretapping.

Ted, who had already returned from Las Vegas, went first, confident in the power of his observation and the force of his analysis. "The two paint tones of the wire clearly don't match, and that doesn't make sense. And there is no way that plaster molding could be perfectly intact in one area and showing plain signs of rot in another a few inches away."

Then Julian, who was best friends with Ted, chimed in. "It definitely looks like somebody was doing something to that wire."

Then Emma, who rarely said anything in public, spoke up. "I really do believe I've been hearing funny noises every time I pick up the telephone."

It was an inspiration to Tony, who transported the suspect telephone from a stand in a corner of the living room to the center of the dining table. "I've been hearing those noises too. It sounds like a buzz or a beep. It starts right after you pick up the telephone, but if you listen for it, you can hear it.

"I want everyone here to make at least one telephone call and then immediately listen for a buzzing or beeping sound. Make sure you don't say anything while calling about being wiretapped, because if they hear you, they'll turn off the equipment right away."

Excusing himself to take a bath because his blood pressure was "a million degrees," Tony went upstairs, pursued by Emma, who wanted to be ready in case cold compresses were required to be pressed on his forehead.

For an hour each of them made not one but several arbitrary telephone calls, listening carefully for the telltale symptomatic buzzing or beeping, and then heatedly debating their findings. They might have gone on deliberating indefinitely the question of wiretapping had not the ringing of the front doorbell startled them—not only because they had worked themselves into a state of paranoid vigilance and were therefore inordinately jumpy, but because no one could remember anyone bothering to knock before, let alone ring a doorbell.

And they were right to think it special, because there was Mr. Sullivan, a thirty-year veteran of Pacific Telephone Company, laden with a huge leather satchel crammed with sophisticated electronic detection devices, responding with the utmost seriousness to the complaint of illegal wiretapping registered by Tony West, who, refreshed by his bath, seemed gratified to see him.

Reiterating his charges, Tony walked Mr. Sullivan through the house and around to the rear, carefully pointing out the evidence of wiretapping he had accumulated. Mr. Sullivan, who seemed determined to get to the bottom of it, listened thoughtfully and carefully considered what he heard. He then returned to the living room and proceeded to attach some instruments to the telephone. He examined the wiring up close in the basement and traced its extension throughout the two-story house. Then he returned to register the readings recorded by his instruments. Only at the end of his exhaustive inspection did he pull up a chair and offer the conclusion he had drawn from his findings.

"I can't say whether the wire or molding you pointed out in the back of the house has been touched in any way. But I find no evidence of wiretapping. I don't hear any buzzing or beeping, and my machines definitely indicate that your lines are free from electronic interference or wiretaps of any kind. I can tell you that now, Mr. West, your telephones are *not* being tapped. If you want me to come back, however, at a future date, I'll be happy to do so."

Visibly saddened and perplexed by these results, Tony stared quietly at Mr. Sullivan. "Are you sure?"

"I'm sure."

Tony thanked him for his time, warmly shook his hand, and escorted him to the front door. There was a hush, a realization, and a dread in the room when he returned that deepened as he addressed them.

"I want everyone to sit here until I come back. I've got to take another bath. My blood pressure's a million degrees again. What I have to say may be the most important thing I've ever said to you."

During the next thirty minutes, sensing the gravity of the situation, no one ventured to leave their seats, and so heavy was the pall that descended that it was a palpable relief when Tony returned.

It didn't matter that he was shirtless, looked unnaturally pale, and inexplicably was carrying a pitcher full of ice-cold water, which he wearily and ceremoniously deposited on the table.

"Obviously they turned off the wiretap before Mr. Sullivan came, and that means they saw him coming. Since they could not have known when he was coming, there is only one way and only one explanation for how that could have happened."

Leaving his chair, he assumed a lookout position by a corner of the large living room window.

"Do you see that green and white truck down the block? It says Barry Exterminating. Well, it's been there two days, and don't tell me it takes two days to exterminate a few houses on the block. That's where they're watching us from."

So mesmerized were the others that they had automatically crouched behind Tony to check out the dubious truck, and just as reflexively now followed him back to his seat.

"I feel that the Frontiersmen are in real danger, and something must be done. Somehow, probably through the wiretap, they've learned that I've figured out who killed Kennedy, and that I'm the only one in America who has the balls to blow the whistle on them.

"Our only hope now, before they close in, is to get our story out to the American public. So I've made a decision. You don't know this, but I've been on a water fast for the past thirty hours, and I'm staying on it until someone *in authority* in the White House at least listens to and acknowledges what is being done to us."

Getting up from his chair, Tony walked over to the fireplace mantel and again retrieved the ax, setting it precisely in place, as though it were silverware, beside the pitcher of water.

"Also, I've sworn a sacred oath, upon my very honor as the leader of the Cult of the Frontiersmen, that unless there is official recognition of our danger from the White House within forty-eight hours, then, as a symbolic protest, *I am going to cut off a finger.*"

Matthew, who had observed longer than anyone the many faces and moods of Tony West, had never seen this one—and he did not have the slightest doubt (nor did the others) that unless these extraordinary conditions were fulfilled, the sacred oath to amputate a finger would be carried out on schedule.

The long and nearly unendurable silence that ensued was shattered by Stuart, who unexpectedly, and with a forced, hollow laugh volunteered, "Take my finger, Tony. Hell, what's one finger! I've got nine more."

Derisively, Stuart wiggled his left forefinger, as though to devalue it while simultaneously perusing his audience for its reaction to his bravado.

Although he did not seem as moved as Stuart had hoped, Tony looked pleased and appreciative. "No, Stuart. It has to be the finger of the leader."

Before departing to undergo his third bath of the morning, he divided the disciples into separate ranks: Bobby, Ted, and Glen in one group; Julian, Cliff, and Stuart in a second group, and Sean, Julian, and Matthew in another.

To his dismay, Matthew discovered the White House to be even more intractable and unreachable than Frank Sinatra, and after literally hundreds of telephone calls during a twenty-four-hour stretch, neither Sean, Julian, himself, nor any of the others had come close to breaking through.

And by the late afternoon of the sixth day, with less than fifteen hours remaining until the deadline, Tony, who had been almost continuously bathing during his prolonged fast, accompanied by his bath attendants, Betty and Emma, bearing another pitcher of fresh ice-cold water, rejoined the others.

It was little more than a day since the proclamation of his Gandhi-like fast, but the effects of his martyrdom were discernible. Tony had lost at least five pounds, and as he tried to resume his customary position at the head of the table, glancing plaintively around him, it seemed even to his most diehard supporters that he was nearing the end of his tether as a leader, and as a man.

Convinced that what they were now fighting to save was a life and not a finger, Matthew, Sean, and especially Julian (who seemed the freshest) furiously renewed their assault on the inner recesses of the elusive White House.

And it was Julian who, in what seemed no less than a miracle to everyone in the room, finally broke through.

"Yes, this is Colonel Tompkins of the United States Intelligence Information Agency. Who is this?"

"Uh, Julian Taggart, of Tony West Enterprises. Did you get my previous messages concerning our harassment, sir?"

"Yes, I did. You say that you are being spied on?"

"We believe our telephone has been tapped and that we are presently under electronic surveillance."

"Why do you believe that, Julian?"

"We have direct evidence of tampering with our telephone lines, which we've reported to a Mr. Sullivan of the Pacific Telephone Company."

"Did Mr. Sullivan check your lines?"

"Yes, he did and he's coming back to continue the investigation."

"Julian, what do you think is the reason that your telephone lines are being tapped?"

Intuitively, Julian, who was less inflexible than Bobby, made the shrewd decision to delete Lyndon Baines Johnson from his explanation.

"Mr. Tony West has been investigating the murder of John F. Kennedy for a number of years. He has some fresh evidence and new ideas which he's writing about now."

There was a pause for the first time at the other end of the line. "Julian, do you think Mr. Tony West could be kind enough to send me, for my records, a copy of that writing?"

"Yes, he will. But Colonel Tompkins, could you please, for our peace of mind, make a record of this conversation so that it won't be lost?"

"I'll not only do that, Julian, but I'll have someone from my office call you tomorrow to confirm it. And you will send that new information on the assassination of John F. Kennedy?"

"Yes, Colonel, we will."

Throughout the exchange, there had been murmurs of "Thank God" and "It's over," and by the time Julian had hung up, he had for a fleeting moment achieved the status of cult hero, the man who had saved the finger, and possibly the life, of Tony West, who, to celebrate the end of the fast, poured himself a glass of Chablis.

Unlike on the previous two nights, Matthew could barely sleep. The possibility of having to witness the live amputation of a finger—whether Tony's, Stuart's, or some other unlucky disciple's—had sickened him. Afterward, lying in bed, he had tried to picture in his mind the sequence of such a procedure: the instrument, no doubt, was to be the short-handled ax and Tony, just as certainly, would have insisted on having a volunteer cut off his finger. Or perhaps, if he had really been driven into a corner, if the stipulated forty-eight hours had expired without the requisite acknowledgement, he might have accepted, as an eleventh-hour reprieve, the heroic gift of a finger from Stuart. One thing Matthew was sure of: No matter how much pressure he was put under, no matter how many fingers were actually amputated, under no circumstances would he offer to sacrifice his own flesh.

Somehow Matthew knew that as much as he had already borne, as Spartan as he had undoubtedly been, he could not have withstood the immolation of his skin, his blood, his bone, and resolved in his mind that he was now prepared to stand watch and defend to the death at least his corporeal integument. He was finally able, in the early morning hours, to drift into sleep.

Throughout everything he experienced and endured in California, Matthew would record but a single dream, a murky one at best, dreamed on this sixth night. A dream without images, colors, or sounds. A dream purely of sensation and feelings, which Matthew would describe as taking place somehow entirely within the domain of his skull and the geometry of his brain. He had never in his life remembered such a dream, wherein it seemed that a tremendous internal tug-of-war between separate parts of his mind and head was furiously being waged. And so real was the tension, so vivid the agony, that long after he had awakened, as he sat upright and panicky in his bed, he could not banish it from his mind.

On the morning of the seventh day, Matthew understood for the first time that the string of imminent but near-miss catastrophes could not continue. Something very soon had to buckle, and break apart: either his sanity or this unbelievable reality he was miraculously still involved in and seemed curiously destined to live out. What the dream told Matthew was that in spite of devastating pressures, his sanity was going to hold together.

It meant, therefore, that these strange doings, this alien reality that he had been getting sucked into deeper and deeper since coming to California with Tony, could not possibly go on, and bolstered in his resolve to stay intact and survive at any cost, Matthew felt confident he could weather the disaster that was sure to come.

In this he was a prophet. At five o'clock on the seventh day, Tony West abruptly called for an emergency meeting of all the Frontiersmen in the living room of Emma's house. If possible, he looked sicker, paler (although he was again eating and drinking regularly), and more desperate than he had been even at the peak of yesterday's fast. Dispensing with any prefatory explanation of the radical action he was about to undertake, he simply announced that, as he had suspected, neither Mr. Sullivan of the Pacific Telephone Company or Colonel Tompkins of the United States Intelligence Information Agency had called back, which meant they had both been spies or plants. Tony returned to his lookout position by the side of the living-room window and pointed to the green and white truck marked Barry Exterminating that was still parked down the block. Then he went to the front door and angrily flung it open.

"Do you see that high rise? That's where they are. That's where the assassin is. Barry Exterminating is just a phony plant to throw us off. I want everybody to come over here."

As though on cue, Emma and Betty emerged from the kitchen, each carrying a tray filled with glasses, cups, and empty beer bottles.

"I'm going to blow the whistle on them. Everybody take a couple of these, and when I say 'Fire,' start pitching them into the street. Now follow me."

Selecting each position as precisely as though he were implementing a military battle plan, Tony arranged the disciples: some on one side of the lawn, some on the other, some on the front porch, and some nearer to the sidewalk.

Then, when he was satisfied, and at a predetermined signal which only he could react to, Tony screamed, "Fire!"

And to Matthew's amazement, all of the disciples, like loyal soldiers, responded with a cascade of cups, beer bottles, and glasses hurled into the spotless, serene street. All of the disciples, that is, except himself—perhaps, as he rationalized, because the limit of his own courage had been reached when he was asked not to help, rescue, or be loyal to a friend, but aggressively to invade the territory of an innocent stranger.

So Matthew let the beer bottle slip from his hand and did not worry about being detected by Tony, for Tony, standing on the top step of the front porch had begun to scream as he commanded "Fire!" and he had not stopped screaming yet.

Was Tony actually attempting to reach the ears of the suspected assassin on the roof of the high rise some three hundred yards away? If he was, he had an awfully good chance of succeeding. There was something awe-inspiring about his rage, as though it originated from some transcendent realm of archetypal pure hatred. From across the street Matthew could begin to see faces gathering in the windows of houses. From the torrent of words, he could only remember three, "Lyndon Baines Johnson," and from the ferocity of its utterance he sensed that in Tony's mind, by so boldly blowing the whistle on a former President of the United States, he was effectively collapsing the structure of American society.

Matthew shuddered at the thought that through his undeniable bond with Tony West he was a part of this terrifying assault on a people and a country he did not have the slightest intention of harming, and he involuntarily took a few steps backward. Out of the corner of his eye, he had seen a horror-stricken Sean go through the motions of tossing a cup a few feet in front of him, deliberately well short of the targeted street, and quickly sneak back into the house. Betty and Emma seemed petrified, rooted to their designated spots, as did Cliff, Glen, Julian, and Ted. That left Bobby and Stuart to be accounted for, and as Matthew began to wonder as to their whereabouts, he noticed a wisp of black smoke slowly climbing above the roof from somewhere behind the house. Matthew ran into the backyard: nothing could surprise him now, not even the sight that met him of Bobby and Stuart, with a look of brainwashed determination on their faces, tending a huge bonfire they had apparently been instructed to light at the signal "Fire!"

With a clenched jaw, as though to menace Matthew in case he had ideas of interfering, Stuart explained, "Tony says we have to keep building the fire until the police come."

According to the sirens, they had already arrived. Fearful that his absence, if detected, would be branded an act of disloyalty, Matthew hurried to retrace his steps—followed by a now openly frightened Stuart and Bobby, who hastily decided they had fulfilled their obligation—and rejoin the others who, incredibly, had not moved.

He felt relief at the spectacle of four police cars parked in front of the house and half a dozen uniformed officers milling around on the front lawn. There would have to be a confrontation now, a resolution of one kind or another, and it would be over. Fate would have taken the matter out of his hands, and there would finally be nothing left for him to do. Trying to take a rapid inventory of the bizarre situation, Matthew knew that Sean, Bobby, and Stuart were hiding in the house, so he did not miss them, but he could not explain the mysterious absence of Tony.

Lacking the one man who could direct them, and therefore afraid of giving a wrong answer to the policemen's questions, the others said nothing, and instead glanced helplessly at the open front door. And Matthew could see that the policemen were nearly as confused as they were; deprived of the usual cues as to the identity and motives of the alleged perpetrators—after all, they certainly did not look like hippies, political activists, radical psychotics, drug users, or criminals—it was hardly clear how to proceed. So it was as much a relief for them to detect the flames from the bonfire, and immediately dispatch several of their number to extinguish it, as it had been for Matthew to note their arrival.

They were even more relieved at the appearance of Tony, whose elegant dress and manner left no doubt as to who was in charge, and therefore responsible. With majestic calm, as though the knowledge he possessed concerning the Kennedy assassination was so potent that it rendered him impervious to any military or police force, he descended the porch steps and strolled into the center of the swarm of policemen.

"What can I do for you, gentlemen?"

"Are you the owner of this dwelling?"

"Yes, I am."

"Are you the one responsible for the bonfire in the backyard?"

"I am aware of no bonfire."

"Are you responsible for the throwing of glass and debris into the street?"

"Oh, that! That was just some housecleaning that got out of hand."

Matthew's heart sank as he realized that Tony was not above outrageous leg-pulling, even with the police, and when he saw an officer begin to reach for Tony ("Listen, wise guy") he automatically raised his arm too—not as a gesture of interference, but as a move toward appeasement. And it was the first major mistake Matthew had committed since arriving in California, if only because he gave the police what they wanted—an open shot at a clear target.

Almost instantaneously with the lifting of his arm, Matthew felt himself strangled from behind by a billy club viciously pressed against his larynx, and before he could grasp what was happening, he was pulled backward and down to the sidewalk by an overeager policeman. Matthew knew exactly how to calm him down. "You win, officer. I'm not resisting. You don't have to strangle me anymore."

For the first time in his life he had handcuffs placed on his wrists, and when he was allowed to get back on his feet he saw that Tony, as well as Glen, who to his knowledge had not said or done anything whatever, were similarly handcuffed.

They were taken in separate cars to the police station, and about halfway there, feeling emboldened and a bit cocky at his newly acquired status as a suspected desperado, Matthew lodged his initial complaint against incipient police brutality. "These handcuffs are hurting my wrist."

"Oh, that's too bad, isn't it?"

Within thirty minutes the romance was over, and the reality of being charged with a crime and treated as a criminal began to sink in. He was a prisoner. No one had the slightest respect for him as a person. He was less than a second-class citizen, he was a citizen without rights, or with rights so marginal (the right, for example, to make one phone call) that he had to be instructed as to their existence.

By the time he had arrived at the police station his survival instincts were in full swing, and he had already learned that by speaking articulately, politely (everything he said either began or ended with "officer"), simply, calmly, and nondefensively, he could defuse at least some of the belligerence that traditionally separated the policeman from his prisoner.

Inside the police station the handcuffs were removed so that he could be identified, searched, fingerprinted, and statistically registered (it was the experience of being fingerprinted, like an indelible biological imprint of your shame, that he would most remember). Then Matthew was marched into an interior room, introduced to a Detective McGuire, and actually allowed to sit, without handcuffs, in an ordinary hard-backed wooden chair, which, given the circumstances, seemed like a luxury. In the center of the room, about fifteen feet to his right, sat Tony in a similar chair, but with his hands still handcuffed behind his back.

Detective McGuire, who had been attempting to conduct a routine interrogation of the man considered to be the prime perpetrator, was having no luck at all, and Matthew could see why. He had seen Tony rational, irrational, murderously enraged, preposterously boastful, diabolically scheming, but he had never seen him speaking gibberish. Yet that is what he was doing now: alternately singing ("Swing low, sweet chariot ..."), reciting psalms ("The Lord is my shepherd, I shall not want"), quoting from his favorite philosophers, speaking in neologisms, and apparently responding to voices that no one else in the room could hear.

No matter what had happened, no matter what was going to happen, Matthew did not ever want to see Tony like this, and he became hopeful when, for the first time since he'd came into the room, Tony, momentarily falling silent, seemed to register and take in his presence.

Perhaps drawing strength from this surprise reunion with his right-hand man, Tony raised himself up in his chair and with his head indicating Matthew, challenged the detective.

"McGuire. See that man over there?"

The detective nodded.

"He's a tough man."

After pausing for a brief appraisal, during which Matthew tried not to squirm in his chair, Detective McGuire snickered, "He doesn't look so tough to me," and then, deciding he was wasting his time waiting for a communication breakthrough, and becoming impatient with what he considered an uninteresting mental case, he gave a signal that the prisoner be removed from his presence.

Immediately a policeman came up behind Tony in order to slide his arms from the back of the chair and help set him on his feet, but no sooner had a hand been placed on his shoulder than Tony, absolutely terrified, whirled to see what was happening. "Are you going to beat me now? Are you going to beat me? I can take a lot."

Shaking his head sarcastically, as though confirmed in his diagnosis, Detective McGuire replied, "We don't beat people here."

Matthew felt guilty that he was so relieved to see Tony led out of his sight, but at least he now had a chance to think. He had no doubt that neither of them was in danger of being beaten by the police, and when he was brought to a single, unoccupied cell it seemed almost a comfort; in some ways it was safer, more private and peaceful, to be here than outside. He tested the sturdiness and thickness of the bars, as do most prisoners, surveyed the sparse confines and contents of his cell, and then tried to relax by sprawling on the lone item of furniture, his cot.

He was actually asleep, as soundly as if he had been in his own bed, when at two in the morning he was rudely summoned. He awoke in darkness to a voice telling him that he had a visitor. He dressed quickly and was taken through some corridors to a narrow room furnished with cubicles. At one of these, he was instructed by the officer who had brought him to be seated. Still rubbing his eyes, Matthew peered through a glass partition at a man whom he had never seen before.

"I'm Barney Simon. I'm your bail bondsman. Your bail has been posted. I'm going to get you out of here."

Within twenty minutes he had signed for his personal effects and magically been regurgitated into the free world. He was greeted outside like a returning hero by Betty and Emma, Ted, Stuart, and Bobby, and could not help being touched by their heartfelt rejoicing. He shook hands gratefully with Barney Simon, a tough-looking former prizefighter, who advised him of the date of his scheduled hearing and sternly but briefly lectured him on his forthcoming legal obligations.

On the way home in the car, surrounded by loving friends, Matthew felt better than he had for a long time. He never wanted to remember the image of Tony speaking gibberish, and he fought to quell panic at the thought that perhaps the nightmarish day had shattered his mind—but when the silence surrounding his name had become ominous, he was compelled to ask, "What about Tony?"

Emma started to cry. "They actually charged him with reaching for the gun of a policeman."

Then Ted, logical as ever, explained: "By increasing the seriousness of the charge, they could raise the bail high enough so that we couldn't get him out before the hearing."

"Those bastards," fumed Stuart.

* * *

So fast was the tempo of events that Matthew could no longer count the days. It was the ninth day, according to the date for the scheduled hearing of the charges against Tony Patrano—but if that were the case, then an entire day had passed in a blur.

All that Matthew remembered of it was this:

His sadness and confusion to discover that Sean, his wardrobe and dresser drawers stripped clean, had taken off, last seen in the fleeing company of Cliff and Julian (they had lasted only a week), who were also reported still missing.

His angry shame upon learning that his bail money had been furnished, via Western Union, by his mother in the Bronx.

And his dismay at the punitiveness of the renowned father of Glen, who, upon being apprised of what had happened and piteously solicited by Betty to bail out his son, had slammed down the telephone, screaming, "He's better off in jail, away from the bunch of you!"

By contrast, the ninth day was burned in his memory. Matthew sat with the others, among the spectators, and waited until Tony was led by the bailiff into the prisoner's dock in a municipal courtroom in downtown Los Angeles. After reading the charges against him, the presiding judge, Clara O'Shay, inquired as to how the accused wished to plead. Matthew sucked in his breath: Would Tony continue to speak in gibberish, as he had to Detective McGuire?

With his hands folded before him, Tony had been studying the face of Judge O'Shay as though straining to grasp the meaning of her words, and when he felt he sufficiently understood the gravity of her question, he bowed his head in order to reflect upon the answer he should give.

"Your Honor, I felt ... after Mr. Sullivan lied about the wiretap, and I saw the assassin on the roof of the high rise ... that if I screamed loud enough about the Kennedy assassination ... so that even the assassin could hear ... it would ... would scare them off ..."

Judge O'Shay, who had been listening thoughtfully, turned to the bailiff, and in an almost compassionate tone asked, "Uh, has the defendant had a mental test conducted?"

After briefly reviewing his docket, the bailiff shook his head.

"Then I think we should have one."

Three days later (Matthew thought, but was not sure, that that was the minimum time required to determine whether a defendant was mentally competent to stand trial), they met in a different courtroom to learn the results of the examination. Something about the legal mechanism by which an individual is deemed sane or insane fascinated Matthew, and he became engrossed, while he waited for Tony's case to be called, in the fate of a man sitting quietly in the dock, a man whom he had never seen before and whose name he could not remember. From the glassy, expressionless eyes, the air of being trapped in a private world, he suspected that the man was insane. Unlike Tony, who had refused a lawyer, this man had legal representation, and when the court-appointed psychiatrist took the stand to testify, the attorney attempted to undermine his expertise.

"You've called the defendant a transvestite. Can you give us the definition of a transvestite?"

Without hesitation, the psychiatrist, a balding black man who looked exceedingly confident and knowledgeable behind his thick-rimmed spectacles, replied, "A transvestite is someone who cross-dresses for sexual pleasure."

After several further questions, easily fielded by the psychiatrist, the presiding judge asked for the results of his mental examination of the defendant.

"The defendant is a paranoid schizophrenic. He is therefore not mentally competent to stand trial for the crime for which he is accused."

A few minutes later, the case of the *State versus Tony Patrano* was called. When Tony appeared, Matthew found himself anxiously scanning his face, especially his eyes, to see if he could detect a comparable glassy vacuousness. It had been four days since he had seen Tony up close, and while he certainly did look different— with his head bowed, he seemed weirdly tranquilized—Matthew could not be sure what the difference meant. He wondered how the psychiatrist, whose imperturbable self-assurance, especially under cross-examination, he admired but did not quite believe in, could determine in a matter of days what he, an intuitively astute observer of human nature in his own estimation, had been unable to achieve in over three years: to fathom the riddle that was Tony's mind.

Yet that is exactly what this same psychiatrist, again taking the expert witness stand, was going to do; and what the judge, after citing the charge and noting that the defendant had declined legal representation, apparently felt he was qualified to do, for he wasted no time in inquiring as to the result of his psychiatric examination.

"I find this man mentally competent to stand trial for the charges preferred against him."

The celebration that greeted Tony, who was pronounced free to go—in four days the bail money, though high, had been raised—was notably subdued. Everyone sensed that he would probably be angry at the disciples for not having bailed him out sooner, and they were frightened what he might do.

But all Tony said, by way of rebuke, was, "What took you guys so long?" And then, with a wave of his hand, "Come on. Let's go home."

Not only was Tony no longer speaking gibberish, but, as Matthew unhappily saw, he was once again completely taking charge of everyone's life.

On the morning of the thirteenth day Matthew was awakened by a long-distance telephone call from his brother, whom he had not spoken to since his visit months ago to California.

"Mother told me what happened."

"I figured she would."

"So what's going on?"

"I have a hearing date, at which I expect the charges to be dropped."

"Everybody threw glasses into the street and Tony started a bonfire in the backyard?"

"Who told you that?"

"Sean and Cliff."

Instantly Matthew became defensive. "What are they saying about Tony?"

"Never mind what they're saying, Matthew, this is insane, isn't it?"

"Well, Tony thinks his telephone is being tapped, and that there's a conspiracy against him."

"Doesn't that sound crazy to you?"

"I don't say I believe it, but I don't think he's crazy, Conrad."

"Matthew, I want you to listen to me. Tony is *insane*. He is clinically insane. I know you love him and he's your idol, but unless you accept this, people out there could get killed."

"Oh, really? As a matter of fact, for your information, Tony was examined by a court-appointed psychiatrist just yesterday, and pronounced legally sane."

"Those asshole court-appointed psychiatrists don't give a shit about real people's lives, and they'll say anything. Besides, Tony's smart enough to twist one of them around his finger."

"Yeah, but he can't fool Conrad the psychiatrist, right? Where do you get off calling him insane when you've spent only one day out here?"

"It's obvious to any intelligent, sensitive person."

"Not to me, it isn't."

"Matthew, listen. You've always been more subjective and emotional than I am. I am telling you I am certain he is insane."

"Fuck you, Conrad. I'm not talking about this anymore."

Matthew hung up the phone, more determined than ever that he would see this thing through to the end, and that no matter what, he would not join Julian, Cliff, Sean, and Conrad in the ranks of the defectors. Restored by the three-day moratorium during which Tony had been in jail, he reasoned with himself he could handle whatever lay ahead.

He had been told to see Tony as soon as he awoke, and getting out of bed, he dressed quickly. Walking through the backyard divider to Emma's house, he had no trouble making a decision not to tell Tony about Conrad's telephone call. Increasingly he was feeling more comfortable holding things back, shading the truth, or downright lying. He could agree with Conrad on one thing, that if anyone could keep Tony from going over the edge and dragging the others with him, it would be Matthew. But he could never lump everything Tony had said, done, and thought into the one word "insane," and then use it to dismiss him coldly, as his brother had done. After all, Tony's life *was* his mind, and for the three most important years of Matthew's life it had been the lode star and reference point upon which he unfailingly depended: the thought of its being in a state of permanent ruin, as Conrad had arrogantly insisted, was too despairing to bear.

As usual, the back porch door was open, and Matthew walked into the house. Emma was in the kitchen, probably cooking breakfast, and Betty was sitting in the living room with her hands folded, looking like an insecure, unwanted guest. He hurried up the steps to see what lay in store, and whether this day would be any better than the others. In the bedroom Tony, who had just finished taking a bath, was buckling on his pants and slipping into a short-sleeved shirt. Smiling pleasantly, he gestured for Matthew to take a seat, and then, with that air of contemplative seriousness, as though he were about to explicate a timeless and profound philosophical conundrum, that Matthew had always revered, Tony began to unburden himself to his right-hand man.

"You know, Matthew, I once defined a great man as someone who denies himself nothing. That is, nothing that is necessary for his greatness.

"When they were holding me in detention, plotting to find a way to have me declared insane so that they could destroy the Frontiersmen forever, I knew if I got out things would have to change. I would have to have what I needed, and take what I wanted. And now is the time to do it."

Tony got up from his chair, and with a childlike look of excitement, placed his hand on Matthew's shoulder.

"Matthew, do you know what I've decided, at long last, to call myself? My new name from this day forth, that all of the

Frontiersmen must call me by, and that when we burst on the scene I shall be known as?"

Uneasy at the direction the conversation seemed to be taking, Matthew smilingly protested, "I thought you were happy with Tony West."

"TONY THUNDER, Matthew! Isn't that great? Until this day I didn't have the balls to call myself that—I thought people would laugh at me. But now, after everything that I've had to go through, I've earned it."

"Look, Tony, I ... uh ..."

"Tony Thunder, call me Tony Thunder."

Matthew sighed, afraid to reveal how ridiculous he thought the name was, and how embarrassed he felt for both himself and his friend.

"OK, Tony Thunder."

Sensing his right-hand man's reservations but refusing to take them into account, Tony smirked, "I see it makes you neurotic. But don't worry, you can still call yourself Matthew, if you like, when we become famous."

"Is that why you wanted to see me? To tell me about your change of name?"

"No. I just wanted to tell you that. The reason is Betty. You saw her on your way up, didn't you?"

"Yes."

"Well, she's driving me crazy. Ever since I brought Emma here, Betty has been falling apart. I thought dividing time between the two houses would make her happy. But nothing satisfies her. I need your help."

Mathew nodded, not having the faintest clue as to the kind of help Tony required.

"I would like you to take her off my hands. Unless she had somebody she liked, I don't think she could ever wean herself away from me. But she likes you."

"I don't understand, Tony."

"Tony Thunder." He smiled slowly, relishing the impact the bomb he was about to drop would have on Matthew.

"I want you to start screwing Betty."

Although he knew he was not, to buy time Matthew said, "You're kidding."

All business now, Tony leaned forward. "No. That's why Betty is downstairs. I've already had a long talk with her, and she's agreed to do it." Then turning toward the bedroom door, as though to substantiate his claim with physical proof, he called out in a loud but calm voice, "Betty, come up here."

Not once in the three years he had known her had Matthew felt sexually attracted to Betty, and even if he had, he would not have been able to perform in a situation that struck him as perverted. But he did not know what to do. Tony, attributing his reluctance to a lack of libido, offered a quick sexual pep talk. "She's great in bed."

That only made matters worse, and when Betty appeared in the doorway, her tight, serious face leaving no doubt that she was prepared to go through with it, Matthew could feel the perspiration dripping from his armpits and running down the sides of his body. He barely looked at her and did not even smile when she sat down in the chair close by his side, the one that Tony had put there for her.

More and more Matthew felt psychologically paralyzed, and to snap him out of it, Tony called upon a favorite tactic: shaming.

Rising to his feet with mock solemnity, he proclaimed: "I know that you're a prude, Matthew, and don't jump into bed with women unless you've made a commitment. So therefore, by the power invested in me by virtue of being the founder of the Cult of the Frontiersmen, I pronounce you man and wife, and declare yours to be the first official cult marriage. You may now kiss the bride."

Too shy to kiss him, but wanting to show compliance, Betty reached out and took Matthew's perspiring hand.

"I shall now leave you two to the joys of the marriage bed." Feigning deference, a smirking Tony left the bedroom.

For what seemed an eternity but was perhaps only minutes, Matthew and Betty sat holding hands, each wondering what the other was going to do. There was no doubt in Matthew's mind that had he wanted or been able to make love to Betty, she would have neither resisted nor joined him: most likely she would have lain there passively, allowing him to undress her, fondle her, and then penetrate her. But he could not be sure that Tony would not be listening outside the bedroom door, perhaps biding his time until he could barge in at the pinnacle of sexual excitement (and therefore of shame).

In the midst of such dark suspicions, there was a knock at the door, and without waiting for a reply Tony reentered the bedroom. He did not seem at all surprised, amused, or angry to find Betty and Matthew sitting inertly side by side, and as though he had already lost interest in the reassignment of his girlfriend to a substitute boyfriend, with a swift shake of his head he abruptly dismissed Betty.

At no time since his arrest had Matthew been so frightened, and never since he had met Tony had he felt so sexually intruded upon and exploited. Yet, judging from the peculiar intensity of Tony's expression, in another of those extraordinary mood swings, the exploitation might not be over.

"Don't worry about Betty. Any time you want her, you can have her. I have something much more important to talk to you about.

"Matthew, it's coming to a head. There's going to be an explosion. I can feel it. I can feel the power of the forces arrayed against me. But we are going to win. It's a superhuman, impossible task, one man and a handful of loyal disciples against the entire government, but we can do it. We can do it, because I am the only man in America with the vision and the guts to blow the whistle on them. But Matthew, I can't do this if I hold back. I've got to give myself everything I need."

Matthew froze.

"I've made a decision. I've always talked, from the days of the clubhouse on, about how great it would be to have orgies, real orgies. But I've never really done it. Now I'm going to do it."

Tony removed a carefully folded piece of loose-leaf paper from his pocket, the kind of paper upon which he often would preserve his spontaneous philosophical ideas. "I've thought about it a lot, and I've written down some positions. We'll start off right here in this bedroom with you, Emma, Betty, and I. Then Emma, Betty, and me will go to your house, where we'll be joined by Bobby and Stuart in your bedroom."

Although he dreaded the answer, Matthew felt that he could not bear not knowing. "What are the positions, Tony?"

"Tony Thunder. Never mind, Matthew. I'll tell you just before we start. I'm going to take a bath now. My blood pressure is about a million degrees. Wait downstairs. In about an hour I'll have Emma and Betty come up. When we're ready, I'll call you."

"What about Ted?"

"Never mind about Ted. Look, Matthew, this has to be done. I know it's a big decision. Do you think it's easy for me, always being the one, the strong man who has to make such decisions?"

"What about the others?"

"I've already talked to them, and they agree. You know, Matthew, after you were a Judas to me by siding with Jay, I still took you back in the fold. I was very nice to you. So don't let me down now."

Then, as though to sweeten the pot, Tony whispered, "I know you've always had the hots for Emma. Well, in an hour she's going to suck your cock. Just think about that while you wait."

In a state of subdued panic, Matthew went downstairs while Tony prepared for his bath. It was true that Emma, with her tawny hair and demure cuddly seductiveness, had turned him on (once last January at a birthday party in his honor, she had managed with a simple congratulatory hug to set his flesh atingle), and the suggestion that she lay ready to service him was unquestionably thrilling. But Matthew knew the price would be terrible, and that among Tony's "positions" there were bound to be some that would be unbearable—otherwise why choose to shroud them in mystery until the very last minute? Yet he refused to consider in any detail, just what the shape and content of such unacceptable positions might actually be.

Alone and miserable, Matthew sat at one end of the black

meeting table and tried as best he could to desensitize his sensibilities. So deep was he into his own hopelessness that he was startled when, with about fifteen minutes to go before the orgy was to begin, Stuart breezily waltzed into the living room. Could he really be this cheerful after having been told about the orgy to come?"

"Stuart, do you know about ..."

"The orgy? What the fuck, Matthew, I'm looking forward to it!"

"Do you know why Ted isn't being included in it?

"Ted's gone. He took all his belongings and cleared out late last night."

"Do you know ... do you know what the positions are going to be?"

Stuart straightened his brawny shoulders and delivered one of his desperate, forced laughs. "Fuck the positions. An orgy is an orgy."

Such showboating in the face of disaster was scant comfort to Matthew. Excusing himself from the conversation, he got up from his chair and began nervously pacing through the downstairs rooms (to distract himself from the countdown).

With about ten minutes to go, the voice of Tony, very calm, strong, and clear, ended the wait.

"Come on up, Matthew."

Of every conceivable "position" he might have expected as he timidly pushed open the bedroom door, he had not expected this: Tony sitting in the same chair, dressed exactly the same way as when he had left him nearly an hour ago—except that in yet another mood swing, he seemed nervous and feverish. And where were Emma and Betty, as promised?

"You look white as a ghost. Sit down, Matthew, I've decided to call off the orgy, at least for now. I don't know, everyone seems so upset by the idea. Right now it's just too much pressure, on top of everything else, for me to take on."

Tony wiped at his still sweatless brow and wearily climbed out of the armchair by the side of his bed.

"My blood pressure's still a million degrees. I've got to take another bath. So far as the Frontiersmen are concerned, the important thing is that I take care of my health."

That night Matthew slept more soundly than usual. He knew that he would never join the ranks of the defectors and would continue to remain loyal to his friends, but for the first time he could envision a day not too far off when the torture he was being systematically and inexplicably put through would end.

As soon as Tony awoke, very early in the morning of the fourteenth day, he knew it was time to share his visions with the others, those who had proven their loyalty by not abandoning him, and who would therefore believe him, in spite of how fantastic they sounded. He had first seen them in the dead of night, as he sat waiting on his padded cot for Detective McGuire to come and beat him. It was only a play of light and shadow on the wall of his cell at first, but when he examined it more closely, if he squinted in a certain way, it had drawn itself together into an unmistakable face-like shape: a long, rectangular, gaunt, bearded visage. Initially, as a skeptic and an atheist he had scoffed at the possibility of a visitation from a supernatural world, and to challenge its authenticity and unmask it as a cheap optical illusion, he had stubbornly kept squinting.

Yet just as stubbornly, the face on the cell wall had resisted optical manipulation. Inching closer, along the edge of his cot, he dared to suspend his intuitive disbelief and to explore the features of its countenance with the sincerity and interest that he might accord a transient human face. And when something about the severity of the beard, the angularity of the cheekbones, and most haunting of all, the grieving of the eyes reminded him of his great hero, Abraham Lincoln, he was not only unafraid but electrified. If there were such a thing as a repository for the anima of a great man that in sacred moments, such as the eleventh hour of the agony of a living great man, would reveal itself perhaps to offer comfort—who better than himself to be the recipient? Hadn't he been the one, the first one, who had conceived of the Utopian American Villages: the simple yet revolutionary idea of genius, of returning in earnestness, in reality, and not in poetic fantasy or hollow rhetoric to the pristine spirit of the original autonomous Americans, of America the Beautiful, before it had become polluted with the thousand sicknesses of the industrialism, technology, and corrosive culture and politics of the masses?

The faces seemed to think so. For they were following him around regularly now, and boldly and freely appearing on the walls of corridors, on the ceiling, on the blanket of his cot—and once, as a kind of cosmic jest, on the naked pate of the very psychiatrist who was seeking to subvert his sanity and lock him away forever. Of course the interrogator had failed and the faces, not only Abraham Lincoln's, but the rough-hewn physiognomy of, no doubt, early American pioneers, whose identity, alas, had been lost to history, rejoicing with him, had laughed—and although they refused to speak to him, touch him, or clap him on the shoulder, as he wished, it was enough that, as he could plainly see and feel, they loved him.

It didn't matter, then, that he had felt crushed when his beloved Matthew had betrayed him by allying himself with the assassin Jay, that his disciples were leaving him like rats on a sinking ship, that Mr. Sullivan, Colonel Tompkins, the L.A. police force, Judge O'Shay, and the evil psychiatrist were joining together to hound him: as long as the presences believed in him, and they obviously did, he was invulnerable.

So in his heart he knew it was right, on the morning of the fourteenth day, to tell his Frontiersmen about the faces, and although they would be spooked at first (perhaps thinking it just another of his Machiavellian tricks), he was sure he could get them to see the truth, as he had. Nothing else, it seemed, was as important; and when the messenger arrived, requesting his signature for a certified letter, which had never occurred since he arrived in California, he was hardly interested, and not at all suspicious, as he certainly would have been before the faces had come to him. But now, what difference did it make if he held in his hand an order to vacate the three houses within forty-eight hours following the receipt of the letter, or face the penalty of a forcible eviction by a marshal and his deputies? Did they think that the faces watching over him would be perturbed by anything so paltry as an eviction notice?

It was, then, as though a great weight had been lifted from his shoulders. The mere knowledge of the presences, whether he actually saw them or not, seemed to free him for the first time to pursue his destiny, without fear or paranoia. He was happier than he could remember, his step lighter than ever, when he joyfully confessed to and revealed the wonderful, magical, visionary faces that had been visiting him from another world first to Emma and then to Betty.

Anticipating their resistance, and their understandable cowardice before the most awful and greatest of truths, he patiently, even lovingly, explained. They meant no harm. They were there to applaud and to extol him as a plain, honest soldier passionately engaged in a just and noble cause. It was their cause too. They had only to squint their eyes, to concentrate long enough and hard enough upon any ordinary play of light and shadow, upon the wall, the ceiling, the pillowcase, their own hands, and if they believed, if they opened their hearts as he had opened his heart in that lonely cell in the dead of night, they too would see.

He commanded each of them, he beseeched, threatened, exhorted Emma and Betty, if they loved him at all, to devote themselves to experiencing the faces, so as to share with him his greatest adventure and most triumphant moment.

He left them to find their individual paths to their personal visions, and in a spirit of joyful liberation, circled the block in a penultimate patrol. Within forty-eight hours he would no longer be surveilling the houses, would be leaving them for good and be on his way toward the final leg of his predetermined mission. It occurred to him that his recent incarceration, psychiatric detention, release, and subsequent threat of eviction was the very stuff of journalism; and in yet another epiphany, he rushed to contact the offices of Dick Allen, a local TV personality who specialized in marginal, idiosyncratic characters with unusual stories to tell—

people who had sighted UFOs, made contact with another world, or been persecuted in some extraordinary way.

He was not surprised when Robert Braddock, Dick Allen's assistant, after listening quietly for about twenty minutes, asked if he could drive over and interview him the very same afternoon; and he was even less surprised when holding nothing back and pouring out his heart for several hours, he was forthwith invited to present his story directly to the American public the next day.

Gathering everyone around him, sitting for perhaps the last time at the head of the massive black table, he announced the news: tomorrow he would be making his television debut on the Dick Allen show! And while he was at it, he decided that now was the time to announce the news of his visions to Bobby and Matthew and Stuart, who had not yet heard it. It did not bother him; he rather enjoyed it that they seemed even more frightened than Emma and Betty had been. After all, there was nothing Tony Thunder loved better than spooking his friends, and there was no greater spook than this one—the fact he had beyond question broken through and made contact with another world. So on this great day, the day of his complete liberation, he allowed his imagination to soar higher and more transcendentally than ever before, and he attempted as never before to cast the most magical spell of all on his faithful disciples.

"We haven't scratched the surface yet, and haven't begun to fathom the possibilities of what's really out there. I've always said that great men are strong in ways that people don't suspect, that they have power even they themselves don't know about.

"I've been an atheist and a skeptic ever since I was fifteen years old, and I've always assumed that it would be impossible for me to encounter a so-called paranormal experience that I couldn't swiftly debunk. But after spending four days in a cell and trying every which way to disprove and exorcise those damned faces on the walls, and being unable to do it, I am forced to admit that the so-called supernatural world does in fact exist.

"But I believe that it does not exist for everyone, but only for the privileged few, such as the Frontiersmen. And because great men do tend to have these unsuspected powers, I now think it may be true that some of these untapped powers may actually be supernatural ones."

Tony Thunder paused to let the enormous weight of his words take effect. Then:

"Haven't you ever wondered why, out of all the billions of people on this planet, it was *only us* who were capable of becoming, who actually chose of our own free will to become, Frontiersmen?

"I used to chalk that up to the roll of the dice, to some kind of freakish luck. Now, especially after seeing the faces, I think that perhaps it was not luck at all, that instead it was because of these secret, superhuman powers we did not know we possessed."

Suddenly turning to Stuart, he asserted, "I believe, Stuart, that if you were ever truly to unlock the full potential of your obviously great physical strength, you might literally be able to defeat fifty men in hand-to-hand combat."

Laughing, Stuart flexed his powerful muscles. "That is decidedly possible."

Then turning to his right-hand disciple, Tony said, "And I believe, Matthew, crazy though this may sound, that if any of us could, you would be the one who could actually fly."

Amused, and relieved to be amused, Matthew had gladly joined in. "You mean with my arms and legs?"

"I know you're all trying to make light of what I'm saying because you're frightened, but I'm serious, Matthew. I've always sensed a lightness of spirit, an aerial quality about you, and I believe it might be possible, if you opened yourself fully to the lightness within you, that you could jump off the roof of this house, maybe right now, and fly."

A silence fell over the table. Not the familiar terrified hush that was wont to strike dumb a room full of panicky disciples, but a much more peaceful moratorium, a kind of collective lull during which people if only for an instant contemplated the possibility and narcissistic pleasure of possessing paranormal powers. And it was under such a spell of pixilated fantasy that Matthew had said (and I found so memorable, as I have already recounted at the beginning):

"He asked me if I thought I might be able to fly, and—I know this sounds weird—I wasn't entirely sure I couldn't."

I could not resist saying, "But you could easily have put the fantasy to a test in the privacy of your room, by trying to levitate an inch or two off the floor."

Matthew quickly saw my point. "I didn't want to test the fantasy, I suppose. It was the first one in months that made me feel good."

That evening, on top of a knoll that rose above a small community church, Bobby, Stuart, Emma, Betty, Tony Thunder, and Matthew shared something more than a fantasy: something that seemed to each of them like an authentic paranormal encounter. What had begun as just another nightly patrol of Los Angeles had ended with an incredible group experience. For standing on the crest of the knoll as they stopped to drink in the beauty of an exceptionally clear, starry night, they had all seen it: a single, ordinary-looking star that had gradually detached itself from the others, begun moving in a shimmering way, expanded to about ten times its former size, and then, intensely glowing, unmistakably seemed to float downward toward them. There was no normal explanation. It was not a missile, a beam of light, an aerial object, or a star, although plainly it had started out as one. What was it, then?

To Tony Thunder, it was yet another confirmation of his glorious destiny—this time in the shape not of a face but of a benign extraterrestrial and watchful UFO—and he ecstatically exclaimed, "Gosh! Don't you wish it would come down here and talk to us?"

To the others, with their excited inquiry "Did you see it? Did you see it?" and their breathless answer "Yes!" "Yes!" it was perhaps the proof they had been searching for that they had at last truly been united with their leader in an indisputably mystical experience.

But for Matthew it was a stubborn mystery, the one thing he

could not satisfactorily explain upon his return from California. He did not know whether to attribute it to subliminal clues concerning paranormal phenomena planted earlier in the day by Tony Thunder, or possibly to a collective version of something he had once read about called *folie à deux*. Whatever it was, the fact that he could not differentiate, pigeonhole, and label it left him with an uncanny feeling that perhaps the seemingly supernatural star was somehow a sign that his experience in California had not been wholly in vain; that there had indeed been something magical about it.

He was awakened early on the morning of the fifteenth day by an exuberant Tony Thunder, who could not wait to get his old friend dressed and ready to go. It was no time to be sleeping. It was a day on which Tony Thunder would become famous, when the Frontiersmen would become known throughout America, and when he would smash in one fell swoop the enemies who thought they could uproot him from his home.

"No one drives the lion from his lair," laughed Tony Thunder. Cocky, yes, but more affably ebullient than Matthew could remember him being in a long time; and as they drove together aimlessly, almost playfully, like tourists in downtown Los Angeles, he felt surprisingly reassured.

Suddenly spying a pet shop he had never seen before, Tony parked the car and signaled that his right-hand disciple should enter the store with him. In a mood swing so rapid that it disarmed even Matthew, he marched to the center of the shop and amid a hubbub of pet noises began furiously surveying the hundreds of animal cages.

"Matthew, listen. Do you hear it? Do you hear those cries? Those are the screams of animals in cages, animals in torment because they want to be free.

"Remember this pet shop, Matthew. One day, when I'm rich and famous, I'm going to come back here and buy every one of these animals, and set them free.

"But for now, I'm going to take just one."

Summoning the proprietor, he pointed to a screened rectangular box containing a lively-looking monkey about ten inches tall. He instructed the owner, "We don't want the cage."

"The monkey is liable to bite you without the cage."

"That's all right. Matthew, just take the monkey and hold its head tightly."

Not wanting to think about it too much, Matthew forced himself to grasp the monkey from behind so as to remove it from the cage. Instantly the animal turned its head and bit his hand. He tried again, attempting to seize it more securely, and was bitten a second time. He got it right on the third try: simultaneously squeezing the torso of the monkey in his right hand and with the fingers of his left hand pinioning the head in a fixed position, so as to prevent it from swiveling and biting.

Although he felt bitter and upset that he had to do it, Matthew did do it, maintaining his two-handed grasp of the monkey during the entire ride back. He was bitten only one more time when upon being instructed to let go of the monkey so as to give it the run of the house, he had made the mistake of releasing the head first.

There was no time to brood about it. In less than two hours Tony Thunder would be making his television debut on the Dick Allen show. Everyone departed in order to get ready: Tony Thunder retiring to his room to meditate on how he would appear and what he would say to America, and Matthew to the medicine chest in his bathroom to treat the numerous bites on the back of his hand.

In forty-five minutes they regrouped in front of the remaining car (the other had been sold to raise bail). Tony Thunder looked handsome and dignified in his favorite suit, the one he had worn to announce his plan to "squeeze Frank," and subsequently to greet the police after blowing the whistle on Lyndon Baines Johnson. Perhaps because everyone sensed that so much was hanging on the outcome of Tony Thunder's television debut, the ride to the studio was uncommonly subdued.

Along with Bobby, Stuart, Betty, and Emma, Matthew sat in a section reserved for friends of the guests. It was the first time he had ever been in a television studio of any kind, and he tried not to think of exactly what it was that made a successful guest—and of the infinite number of things that could go wrong.

He was surprised at how big Dick Allen looked in person. About six feet two inches tall, he had thin, reddish hair neatly combed back, a broad face, a nasal voice, and a bemused, pugnacious manner. As was to be expected, he looked completely at home in front of the cameras.

Tony Thunder was to be the second of three guests. The first was a young man who identified himself as the leader of a neo-Nazi White Supremacy party. Inexplicably self-composed, he seemed virtually immune to Dick Allen's attempts to ridicule and unsettle him. Patiently, he explained the key differences between the Nazis of Hitler and his own contemporary version of neo-Nazism. He enumerated the reasons that made white supremacy not only a viable but a necessary concept in the modern world, and he outlined a number of detailed proposals to implement it.

The audience reaction, surprisingly, was one of morbid curiosity. They acted as though they were witnessing the tragic spectacle of an intelligent, clean-cut, well-spoken, and generally likable young man who had only one thing wrong with him: somehow, somewhere along the line, something had turned him into an evil and insane person.

Astutely reading the fascinated mood of the audience, Dick Allen allowed his compelling first guest to remain onstage for nearly half of the show's allotted time, at the end of which he made a pretense of humanitarian concern for a man gone bad.

"You're obviously an intelligent, capable person who could have had a number of successful careers. What made you choose a thing like this?"

"I know my choice is not a popular one. But I love my country, and this is the best way I know of serving it."

The applause was muted and pitying. It was time for the next guest. Matthew took a deep breath. For most of the past thirty minutes he had been feeling increasingly anxious, not only because he hated Nazis but because he intuitively realized that the combination of self-proclaimed leader of the White Supremacy Party and eloquent spokesman would be a tough act to follow.

Dick Allen slowly shuffled some index cards in his hand, giving himself time to prepare for his second guest. Then, when he was ready, he faced the audience and announced:

"Our next guest is a man who calls himself Tony Thunder. He is the founder of the Cult of the Frontiersmen, a group of people dedicated to the revival of principles of early Americanism.

"Mr. Thunder believes that because of his unpopular beliefs he has been systematically persecuted, tortured, and imprisoned by local and federal authorities, and he wants to tell us about it.

"Ladies and gentlemen, please welcome Tony Thunder."

Amid restrained applause, Tony Thunder, looking very serious and determined, walked onto the stage.

"Mr. Thunder, maybe we could begin by your telling us why you founded what you call the Cult of the Frontiersmen."

"Yes, Dick. Well, it's based on about ten years of philosophical thought. The essential idea is that there was a certain generosity, freedom, and noble adventurousness of spirit imbuing the early Americans that has been systematically eaten away by the inroads of industrialism, technology, and what I call the corrosive culture and politics of the masses.

"Now, I believe the building of my Utopian American Villages can help restore ..."

"Yes, yes, Mr. Thunder. I understand that the name on your driver's license is Tony Patrano. Is that correct?"

"Yes, it is."

"Could you tell us why you are choosing to be known as Tony Thunder instead of Tony Patrano?"

"Well, names are symbols. I chose Tony Thunder because I think it represents the cataclysmic impact that my Utopian American Villages are going to have on the contemporary consciousness."

"I see. Well, don't you think Tony Thunder and Lightning would have achieved an even greater impact, if impact is what you want?"

"Is that your pathetic attempt at wit, Mr. Allen?"

"No. It's my attempt to understand a curious man. According to my information, your Frontiersmen list two women, a Betty and an Emma, as members. Is that correct?"

"Yes, it is."

"Then why don't you call your cult the Frontiersmen and the Frontierswomen? Isn't that sexist?"

"Mr. Allen, this is about important philosophical ideas, not sexism. There will be plenty of recognition and room for women in the cult."

"You say you've been persecuted by the local and federal authorities. Could you tell us how?"

"Yes. My telephone wire has been tapped. A Mr. Sullivan from the Pacific Telephone Company has verified that. You can check that. A van with electronic surveillance equipment parked itself right outside my house for about a week. They tried several times to psychiatrically detain me, so as to permanently lock me away— but they couldn't."

"And why, Mr. Thunder, do you think you are being persecuted?"

"Because I have figured out that the man behind the assassination of John F. Kennedy was Lyndon Baines Johnson."

"You say on national television that a former President of the United States, whom many of us regard as one of our greatest Americans, is a murderer?"

"I'm not saying that he pulled the trigger, Mr. Allen, or was on the scene, but I do insist he knew in advance about the assassination plot and chose to do nothing about it. Much as Franklin Roosevelt, as has been written about, knew that the Japanese were going to bomb Pearl Harbor, but did nothing."

"Do you have hard proof of this?"

"No, but I ..."

"I think I see why they psychiatrically detained you."

"If you'll stop interrupting me, Mr. Allen, I will explain my reasons."

"Did anyone ever tell you that you drool when you speak?

Maybe this will help."

Dick Allen had unexpectedly reached over, lifted a folded handkerchief from the breast pocket of a startled Tony Thunder, and derisively placed it, like a waiter setting a napkin in place, on the forearm of his enraged guest.

As the audience began to laugh uneasily, Tony Thunder, glancing at the handkerchief as though it were excrement, slowly got up from his chair. Pinching it gingerly between a forefinger and thumb, he hoisted it in the air, examined it for a moment, and then scornfully pitched it back at Mr. Dick Allen (who, to his credit, did not bat an eye).

It happened so fast the audience did not have time to react: Tony Thunder, with a jerk of his arm furiously signaling his disciples to follow him and then haughtily striding off the stage. As one, the disciples, like puppets yanked by a puppeteer, had jumped to their feet and exited in tandem through the crowded studio aisles. For Matthew it was an especially painful humiliation, and, with his eyes lowered in embarrassment until he reached the anonymity of the street, he found himself wondering just how much more he could bear.

Rejoined by his disciples outside, Tony Thunder immediately attempted to repair his damaged prestige. "Dick Allen is just a dumb asshole trying to be a big man in front of the audience. Let's go home."

Matthew realized that within twenty-four hours, now that the so-called last hope of a successful eleventh-hour television debut had utterly fizzled, the marshal and his deputies would see to it that there would be no home. Given that there was only one car and six people, it meant that some of them would be splitting up, at least temporarily. Suddenly the idea of a vacation in his house in the Bronx, cared for by his mother, seemed not only logical but irresistibly attractive. He would never, of course, be a deserter like the others, and he would always be a Frontiersman, no matter what state he lived in.

Once he had given himself permission in his own mind to

return to New York, he couldn't wait until he had reached his house and the privacy of his bedroom, so as actually to telephone his mother, who, as he knew, would be overjoyed at his request. Yes, a ticket would be waiting for him at the L.A. airport tomorrow, and yes, he was welcome to come home. Relieved that he was leaving but anxious as to how to break the news, he decided that a lie would be necessary; he would say he had to see his Aunt Rose, who was dying of cancer, and he resolved that under no circumstances would he allow himself to be talked out of it.

But he would not reveal his plans until the last moment, and when Tony Thunder, with tears in his eyes, walked into his bedroom about twenty minutes after he had spoken to his mother and invited Matthew to accompany him on a farewell tour of the city, he was certain he had made the right decision. Tony was in no shape to receive the news of the imminent departure of his right-hand disciple.

So Matthew would play the role and do Tony Thunder's bidding one more night, and when he was instructed to recapture the uncaged monkey—so as really to set it free before the houses were repossessed—he hardly balked. He hardly listened as Tony talked randomly and grandiosely about plans to start all over again in Mexico, and he hardly reacted when Tony parked the car on the outskirts of a luxurious, fenced-off mansion in a section of town know to be populated with the estates of celebrities.

With a sentimental look on his face, as though he were returning to a beloved haunt, Tony got out of the car.

"This used to be the home of Bing Crosby. You didn't know it, but I would sometimes drive here in the early morning and tell myself that one day I would own it, or a mansion just as great.

"Well, maybe I still will. Anyway, I thought what better place, Matthew, to free the monkey than in these trees."

For once he was happy to comply: with one motion, so as not to be bitten, he simultaneously released and propelled the monkey to the nearest overhanging branch.

Satisfied that a precious ritual of freedom had been initiated and consummated, Tony Thunder put his arm around the shoulder of his accomplice and still right-hand disciple.

"No matter what happens, we'll always be Frontiersmen, won't we, Matthew?"

Matthew nodded, but thought, frightened that his resolve was going to slip away, *Yes, but first I must go to New York.*

When he returned home, following the conclusion of the valedictory patrol of Los Angeles, Matthew discovered that Bobby and his belongings had disappeared. About an hour later Stuart knocked at his bedroom door and anxiously looking behind him, without waiting for a reply entered the room.

"Matthew, listen, I have something to say."

"Yes?"

"I'm leaving."

"I understand."

Suddenly Stuart, who was speaking with more emotion that Matthew had ever seen in him, balled up his fists and shook them in the air as though threatening an unseen opponent.

"I think Tony was the greatest philosopher in the world, and he tried to stand alone against a sick society, but they were too much even for him.

"Matthew, I think they have driven Tony insane! And I'm going to make those bastards pay for it!"

Realizing that beneath Stuart's desperate showboating was a genuine need for some kind of permission to go, Matthew reached over, patted him on the shoulder, and in the same fatherly way that he had advised Jay two weeks ago to consider his own safety first, said, "It's all right. I think you should leave too."

And when Stuart had done just that, visibly relieved at the blessing he had received from the original disciple, Matthew became aware of a subtle but monumental shift in his perspective: Instead of thinking of anyone who wanted to quit the Frontiersmen as deserting, he now thought of him as leaving. For Matthew, who still prided himself on being the most loyal of all, it was a personal milestone.

* * *

On the morning of the sixteenth day, the last day he would spend in California, Matthew dressed quickly. His flight was at night, but he wanted to get it over, had to get it over, so he forced himself one more time to travel the distance that separated the backyards. As promised, the marshal and two deputies were already there, stationed in the living room, silent supervisory sentinels, as Emma and Betty, weepy-eyed, packed what needed to be packed into boxes; everything remaining would be carted to storage. Tony Thunder, resplendently dressed, sat at the foot of the stairway. In his two hands he held a framed picture of his sister Jean, taken when she was a child just before she was first institutionalized at Creedmoor Psychiatric Center.

"They did this to her," said Tony Thunder, believing he had just solved for the first time the riddle of his sister's madness, which had never ceased to trouble him.

Noting his preoccupation with the photograph, at which he had been staring for fifteen minutes, the marshal chided, "You'll have to move along, Mr. Thunder. The storage truck will be here in a couple of hours."

"Oh, right, Chief!" roared Tony Thunder, in an outburst of stentorian rage.

So it was certainly not the best time; it might even have been the worst time, but it had to be done. Taking Tony Thunder aside, Matthew spoke in a low, urgent voice. He was returning to New York to see his Aunt Rose, who was dying of cancer; given the amount of luggage, there would be no room in the car for him anyway; and he would probably be back, when things were resettled once more, in a matter of weeks. Although he had felt the need as a security blanket to lie about his Aunt Rose dying of cancer, he had believed at the time he said it that he would indeed be back after a short vacation.

Perhaps because he was depleted from the humiliation of being forcibly ousted from his three homes, or perhaps he was becoming mellower, but Tony Thunder offered no resistance. Emotionally laying a hand on Matthew's shoulder, he presented his final piece of advice to his original disciple.

"Just remember, Matthew, everyone in New York will be trying to convince you that I am insane. If they can convert you, you will be their prize catch. So keep the faith, and I'll call you at your mother's house."

When Matthew said that he would keep the faith, he believed it at the time, and although he was leaving, continued to think of himself as a loyal Frontiersman, and accordingly was no less emotional than his mentor when they shook hands for the last time.

Matthew arrived at the airport six hours in advance of his scheduled flight back to New York, but it still was not enough to sort out, contain, and understand his racing thoughts, and when he boarded the airplane, he was as confused as ever, albeit somewhat exhilarated. His big question was, roughly, who was he, how should he conduct himself, and how would he be regarded now that he had stepped out from under the magic umbrella of the Cult of the Frontiersmen?

An answer of sorts came around four in the morning when, ignoring the No Smoking sign, he had lit up a Lucky. Almost simultaneously a stewardess, whom he had not seen walking up the aisle behind him, snapped, "Put out that cigarette"—and then, as though to make sure her command would be obeyed, stood waiting, with an impatient glare, beside his seat.

Initially amused, Matthew became progressively hurt, incredulous, and angry. Could she possibly be treating him in this degrading manner? Of course she did not know he was a Frontiersman, but wasn't there some residue of his former persona that would at least shield him from the insults of menial but presumptuous employees such as this woman? The fact that there was not, as he ground out his cigarette, the fact that the months of agony he had been forced to endure in California would count for nothing to strangers, to New Yorkers, to New York City, would be a painful though beneficial lesson that would help him, as much as anything, to reintroduce himself to the real world, neither grandiose nor ungrandiose—the world that just is.

* * *

Generally it takes about a week for someone who has been indoctrinated into a cult and is then effectively removed from its sphere of influence to begin to grasp just how pervasive that influence has been.

For Matthew, it took about three days, in the comfort and isolation of his mother's house. The first day was a dawning of just what he had been through, of the terrible price he had paid for his friendship and loyalty to Tony, and of appreciation for the pleasures of being away from the cult. On the second day he drew up his bill of grievances for all that Tony had done to him in the name of the cause, and allowed himself for the first time to acknowledge his anger and rage toward his immaculate mentor. And the third day was the day of enlightenment and epiphany. Egged on by Conrad, he had decided for the heck of it to reread his college textbook on abnormal psychology. Under a section entitled "Signs of Manic-Depressive Disorder," he had made his electrifying discovery: wild mood swings, incredible flow of energy, intermittent spells of depression, delusions of grandeur (e.g., often considering themselves a soldier of God), hallucinations, belief in the possession of supernatural powers, paranoid ideation often leading to behavior resulting in incarceration—it was all there, and now he himself at last could say it: *Tony Thunder was a manic depressive, and therefore was clinically insane!*

Putting a name to Tony Thunder helped set Matthew free and gave him the courage he desperately needed to make the crucial decision not to return to the Cult of the Frontiersmen. And when, true to his word, about a week after he had come back to New York, Tony telephoned, Matthew found it far easier than he had imagined to signal to his mother that he did not wish to speak to his former mentor.

It was easy, too, not to reply to the letter he received three weeks later from somewhere in Mexico, written in the presumably now lucid hand of Tony Patrano.

The only sentence that mattered to Matthew was this: "I therefore admit that for a period of about two weeks I had what could be clinically described as an (affective) manic-depressive attack, but I want you to know that no matter what I did, I never intended to harm you or any other of the Frontiersmen."

Matthew read it correctly; it was Tony Patrano once again taking charge by delivering his own diagnosis of his undeniably bizarre behavior, and once again attempting to woo back the minds and hearts of his erstwhile disciples.

But this time it would not work, and although Mathew had barely begun to take his own life seriously, he was understandably invigorated to realize that his involvement with the Cult of the Frontiersmen and what he always referred to as his friendship with Tony Patrano were, mercifully, finished.

THE ANATOMY OF A CULT

Although there are many separate factors involved, indoctrination into a cult, to a great extent, is based upon the seduction of impressionable young adults, often teenagers, who are typically attempting to work out a late-adolescent identity crisis (Erikson, 1968).

No fact of cult life is more important, when it comes to the successful indoctrination of new members, than its isolation. Anyone who enters the inner recesses of a cult soon realizes that what is being left behind is the world as we know it, for better or worse. On one level, then, cults are founded upon the same psychology that binds adolescent or delinquent gangs together: the stubborn division of the world between everything out there and the family-like group. Such isolation is achieved and reinforced, in part, by the obsessive and relentless devaluation of everything outside the sphere of influence of the cult, which means everything from pop culture to the fundamental texture of contemporary life. It is aptly summed up in the slogan "Life stinks"—and it was an omen of things to come when Tony Patrano, within minutes of meeting Matthew, began to devalue the processed fast food they both were eating and use it to illustrate his thesis that civilization was in dire need of repair.

But if there is devaluation of the world at large, then its counterpart must surely be the grandiose claims made on behalf of the cult, and especially the person of the founder. Seen in this light, the strange self-assertions of Tony Patrano—that he was a great philosopher, a great lover, a great salesman, a great puncher—that so irritated Matthew were anything but random instances of an annoying braggadocio: they were the necessary cement, the linchpin required to reassure a panicky core of adolescent disciples that they would be richly compensated for the world they were being asked to abandon.

It becomes apparent to anyone being initiated into a cult that there are consequences to be faced for such a choice, and a price to be paid; and it is almost a matter of course that the radical isolation requisite for entry into a cult will carry with it a varying but predictable degree of schizoid detachment, impaired reality testing, and a certain antisocial behavior easily rationalized as idealistically motivated civil disobedience.

One of the most pernicious effects of such isolation, which exponentially increases the deeper one plunges into the heart of a cult, is what may be called psychic numbing to the outside world. Robert Jay Lifton (1983) has eloquently described the psychic numbing that has already occurred, on a broad contemporary front, in regard to the logically plausible but emotionally unthinkable—holocaust that would ensue from a nuclear confrontation. Yet there is a profound difference: the psychic numbing that Lifton depicts can take years or decades to emerge; and its effect is to eradicate from consciousness a portion of reality that is too catastrophic to incorporate.

By contrast, the psychic numbing that is achieved by inclusion in the life of a cult can take place in weeks or months—and what is eradicated is not a portion (however significant) of reality, but the world itself. This is another way of saying that the psychic numbing of a member of a cult is wholesale and not selective, and one of its inevitable effects is to foster a symbiosis to the cult. This means that the world, psychologically, has shrunk to the parameters of the cult, and to someone so involved nothing seems easier or more natural than to place unlimited importance upon the cult. Yet if the cult is thereby to substitute effectively for the world, to justify the claim that it can, it must convincingly stand proxy for much of what outside society provides: job opportunities, education, friendships, social standing. Given its abnor-

mal restrictiveness, this is virtually impossible, and to compensate
for its failure as an effective microcosm, a cult will often resort to
a two-fold denial: psychic numbing, on the one hand, which is
used to devalue everything the cult cannot provide, but the world
can; and on the other hand an unreal, hyperbolic flattery of
members meant to achieve an inflated and soothing sense of the
greatness of the cult.

To the extent that the cult member comes to believe that there
is really nothing out there for him other than his cult affiliation,
a symbiosis cannot help ensuing; and as though to make doubly
sure the member stays in check, the symbiosis that develops is
often enforced (a common tactic of criminal organizations)—
that is, if you ever do decide of your own accord to leave, you will
live to regret it.

Tony Patrano enforced the symbiosis he wanted by frightening
newcomers with gruesome stories of his exquisite talent for
revenge, and it was no accident that the effect was to promote a
paranoid for-us-or-against-us mentality. Such symbiosis was never
so named, but was instead lauded as loyalty to the cult, which in
turn was strengthened by the strategy of instilling in the minds of
members who might be thinking about leaving the twin feelings
of guilt and fear of reprisal.

The symbiosis that arose, then, was especially powerful, with
many ramifications, one of the most important of which was the
impairment of reality testing. There is a contrast between the
noncontextual thinking of the paranoid (Shapiro, 1965), which
inhibits a normal associative draining off of underlying affects
(Freud's catharsis theory, 1895), and cult symbiosis as a kind of
reality repression and denial of reality more commonly found in
psychosis (Freud, 1894). In cult symbiosis, however, the denial of
reality is communally shared, and therefore is more operational
and functional, perhaps in the sense in which Freud (1928)
spoke of organized religion as a shared delusion.

It follows that the fully indoctrinated cult member, on some
level, knows that his functional sanity must depend not only on

his own defenses but on those of his fellow members—which means that without them (i.e., in the event of expulsion from the cult, which is an ever-present possibility), there can be immediate danger of decompensating. This is another way of saying that within the symbiosis of the cult, defenses have become external-ized: and analogous to the way Freud (1922) pictured the ego ideal, in the state of love, as being captured by the beloved, it can be said that in the case of the initiate, such defenses have been similarly captured not by an individual but a cult—and to that extent transformed into group defenses.

In this way, a cult represents a compromise against a threatened psychotic loss of reality: on the one hand, it denies or loses (Freud, 1894) an unbearable outer reality; on the other hand, it reinvents it in a manner that, (unlike with the psychotic), elicits considerable and comforting consensual validation. Consequently, the cult member, no matter how fantastic the set of beliefs to which he fanatically adheres, does not have to put up, as does the isolated, lonely psychotic, with the ridicule and censure of a hostile external reality. In this sense, the radical impairment of reality-testing fos-tered by the symbiosis of the cult—a kind of extended *folie à deux*, as retrospectively intuited by Matthew—in comparison with the psy-chotic's classical denial of reality, is nevertheless significantly more adaptive.

Seen in this light, the rituals of the cult, whatever they are, may be looked upon as a necessary reinvention of reality, and an attempt, however pathological, at restitution process. Yet there are differences between the zealot's sweeping symbiotic dismissal of the world as we know it and the more commonplace psychotic denial: the latter may be accidentally activated by an interper-sonal trigger (as might have been the case with Tony Patrano when he became subject to paranoid fears that he was being betrayed in New York by Emma)—but the stubborn symbiotic loy-alty to the cult, so evident in Matthew, is often aggressively induced by a single grandiose and charismatic individual.

There is a way, then, to think of *folie à deux* as perhaps the end result of a long and runaway process of psychological blackmail:

"Share my madness or I will abandon you"—and the demoralized symbiotic partner who is faced with this most terrifying of ultimatums, may well choose to suffer the loss of the world (reality) rather than sustain the even greater loss of the relationship.

This is not to deny that someone like Matthew was highly predisposed to being converted to membership in a cult, and had already, prior to induction, incurred a considerable loss of inner reality—a deficit of self experienced as a painful void or deadness—that was enthusiastically exchanged for the much more stimulating interpersonal symbiosis of life in a cult. Nevertheless, the symbiosis of the initiate may be seen as a substitute displacement of a preexisting intrapsychic defense against loss to the more glamorously stimulating and manic interpersonal defenses that flourish in a cult.

There is much that follows from this picture. If symbiosis is what is being sought and created, it is understandable that loyalty will be elevated to an indispensable virtue. That the grandiosity of the cult will be a necessary defense to shore up the loss of reality, impoverishment of the ego, and pathologically low self-esteem that must already precede initiation. That cults will often depend on hyperstimulation—"fun," rebellious adventures, more intense pleasure through hedonistic orgies—to cover up inner loss and deadness.

And it follows that cults, to protect the symbiosis they have arduously cultivated, will seek to mask the underlying enslavement of their members by glorifying and shamelessly flattering their autonomy in whatever way possible:

They are "great" because they are members of a great cult.

They are pioneers, because instead of following (*The True Believer*, Eric Hoffer, 1951) the conformist mass media, mass culture world (Ortega y Gasset, *Revolt of the Masses*, 1930), they pledge their wholehearted loyalty to a proud few.

They are courageous, because they are prepared to sacrifice and renounce literally everything for their beliefs.

They are idealistic, because they are staking their lives on principle, and turning their backs on conventionality and economic security.

AMERICA THE BEAUTIFUL

They are autonomous: their decision, because it flies in the face of everything that is popular and acceptable, cannot be the act of a follower, but must be that of a leader.

By a curious twist of logic, they are led to believe the following perverse proposition: since it obviously takes more courage to pursue a course the entire world condemns than to embrace what is universally lauded, to pledge allegiance to a bizarre cult requires more courage than to stay safely in tune with what is called "the real world."

And finally, they are discriminating because the path they have chosen is the path to utopia.

It is a commonplace observation that it is almost impossible to encounter anyone immersed in a cult who isn't grandiose, or whose beliefs or whose leader isn't grandiose in some transparent and typically intrusive way. What is less well understood is the degree to which such grandiosity functions as a defensive bastion against the imminent fragmentation of the group self and the cult identity; and even more remarkable is just how much of this grandiosity can be linked directly to the symbolic but deeply personal expression of a single extraordinary individual.

Charisma

It was the word Matthew used more than any other when he sought to explain the power of his mentor's personality. It came in diverse shapes, but its presence was unmistakable. Muhammad Ali had it, Bjorn Borg had it, Frank Sinatra had it, and, more than anyone he had personally encountered, Tony Thunder, a/k/a Tony West and Tony Patrano, had it.

Charisma, as a psychological quality or emanation, may be thought of as a surcharge of personality or leadership characteristics that fill most easily the emptinesses of another person's psyche: especially those created by boredom, depression, and developmental deficits. Charisma, through its power to overstimulate, can effectively mask the narcissistically seductive and self-serving aims that are often blatantly evident. A collusive bargain of sorts may be struck between the charismatic individual and the person who is seductively charmed, who perhaps has come to think: Maybe I am being manipulated, but it feels so good. I'll go along with it anyway—because I know I am getting something in return.

It is part of the seductive appeal of the charismatic individual that he is spending time in the pursuit of his object, who again may come to believe: Unless there is something unique about me, even if he is using me, he wouldn't be wasting his time on me, since obviously he can have anyone he wants. The fatal flaw in this chain of reasoning is that no one is less discriminating than the charismatic individual, who, like Don Juan, must have whoever is before him: i.e., anyone and everyone. Charisma in this sense, far from being selective, is a promiscuous quality, which through its incessant aggression can cloak the addictiveness of the charismatic person himself as well as the dependency of his object. And charismatic seduction generally works by a tacit collusion of both parties: there is a hidden agenda of denying a covert deadness and passivity of both partners by consummating a relationship that, while meaningless in terms of human intimacy, is exciting.

The action of charisma may be seen as one of the deflection and transformation of inner energies, an energetic involvement of all available psychical powers, which seem to the enraptured beholder to glow and radiate outward into lines of force. Seen in this way, it can seem like an almost perfect preadapted mechanism for manic projection—which may be why manic attacks, no matter how bizarre, psychotic, or disturbing, are to a certain degree charismatic.

Yet the radiance of charisma can be deceptive, and some of the dazzling energy displayed by the charismatic personality may be no more than the forceful manifestation of the psychic work that is necessary for transforming inner affects to outer affects, and therefore may not be so free-flowing as it seems. This is another way of saying that part of the mesmerizing power of the charismatic personality, analogous to the way a magician performs a trick, is that it successfully conceals the struggle that was required to produce it. What is presented instead is only the happy, seemingly effortless, shimmering outcome of an often intense concealed process—Muhammad Ali, for example, psyching himself up in the dressing room before entering the ring—and what is rarely understood is how hard the charismatic person works at being charismatic.

To understand why charisma works as well as it does—given its duplicitous nature, which over time is invariably exposed—it may be helpful to look at *narcissistic giving*, which often occurs when a person wishes to deny, cover up, and defend against an underlying sense that he has nothing of real value to give, by acting as though he is not only giving more than enough, but is in fact giving grandiosely. Part of its pattern is to take what is really a crumb (in terms of true nurturance) and by treating it as though it were a generous gift, thereby to achieve the secondary gain of never having to work on the covert deficit and conflict over giving. And one of the popular strategies of narcissistic giving is the interpersonal one of deflecting the awareness of the recipient (who is being given nothing) from the actual frustrating present transaction by trying to stimulate greed through promises of extravagant gratification in the future.

Thus the charismatic person who seems radiant with the promise of untold flowing riches—but who has little regard for the individual, almost no time and energy to devote to the establishment of a one-on-one relationship, and often seems impaired in his capacity for ordinary human intimacy—is the ultimate narcissistic giver. And if narcissistic giving is his forte, then its counterparts are *narcissistic strength* and *narcissistic honesty*. Narcissistic strength refers to the frequent attempts of people to transmute glaring weaknesses into assets simply through aggressive boasting: as though feeling free repeatedly to reveal what they do (e.g., seduce women) is proof that what they do is thereby worth being reported. Narcissistic honesty refers to the common belief that merely owning up to a negative trait—"Yes, I'm a selfish person" "Yes, I'm very blunt" (meaning hostile)—has simultaneously resolved a conflict: e.g., the woman or man in an unhappy love relationship who thinks that merely announcing, "My feelings have changed, I no longer love you," achieves a wished-for termination with no further work to be done.

It follows that the leader of a cult, who is obsessed with his impact upon others, will not fail to use his personal charisma—his talent for narcissistic giving, narcissistic strength, and narcissistic honesty—to the fullest, and will be especially aware of its effect upon the fragile minds of the would-be devotees who are his primary target. Within these rather extraordinary constraints—only those are susceptible who are predisposed to initiation into a cult—the influence of charisma is awesome; its effects can perhaps best be compared with those of a drug. It is no exaggeration to say that for the true believer in the cult, the charisma of the leader can often function as a euphoria-building, antidepressant drug. In its ability to make one feel good, charisma (in the mind of the believer) can seem a high, and part of the addiction of members to a cult is an addiction to the charisma of the cult. It is easy, then, for the initiate to feel that should he leave, he will be unable autonomously to supply the highs to which he has become habituated. Yet sooner or later, the initiate will leave, (almost all do), and when he does, a pattern of behavior may ensue that will be difficult to distinguish from the withdrawal symptoms of a recovering substance addict: disorientation, paranoia, depression, demoralization, and acute identity crisis.

If one individual, in the person of a founder of a cult, can wreak such havoc, it may be useful to know in advance some of the warning signs of the potentially destructive charismatic personality.

They are:

- An aura of having a significantly greater energetic drive than other people, which does not necessarily derive from an excess of cheerfulness or mania (the popular misconception), but may be the expression of an angry depression—as is often the case with the incendiary leaders of minority groups.
- A sense of a psychic surplus, which cannot help overflow upon others.
- Narcissistic self-absorption, which can seem unremitting, coupled with a self-justifying, sanctimonious identification with a greater goal.
- An ability to draw people to him: for while the charismatic personality is always emitting psychic lines of force, he is also always receiving them, and there is the distinct sense, when in the close company of such a person, of occupying a hublike position in a dynamically charged force field.
- And, as a consequence, the perception that he almost automatically will endeavor to convert whatever group he inhabits into a force field.

You might say of the charismatic person, then, that it is his obsession to be not a self but a personality, to be not larger than life but larger than himself. It is almost as though the normal boundaries of his skin and designated interpersonal space are insufficient to contain a persona so animated, that energy seems to be bursting out of him—and it is understandable that people who come into contact with such an individual often feel they have to get out of the way so as to allow the charismatic personality room to actualize itself. Because of this, there is a fear that to suppress the charismatic persona would not only require too much effort, but would unleash a predictably violent counterreaction: something like getting in front of a speeding truck.

For all of these reasons, the charismatic person strikes us as an embodiment of an archetype, a folk hero such as an athlete, or, on another level, a paradigm of some elemental human force. Because of their greater psychic energy, charismatic personalities seem more primitive, and therefore more connected to their unconscious. It is common upon meeting a charismatic person, much more so than with other people, to feel that one has just come into contact with an unconscious personality. And for this reason, even if he is also acknowledged to be brilliant, the cognitive processing is perceived as having a correspondingly weaker hold on the more dominant unconscious personality, and to be mainly in the service of channeling an insatiable surge of psychic energy.

Instinctively, charismatic people instill in us a for-them-or-against-them attitude, and it is as though we recognize that their personality needs are so enormous that compromise is out of the question. Part of the attraction, therefore, is the opportunity by identifying with them, to attain a sense of release by merging with their vast unconscious personalities. To the disciple who seriously throws in his lot with the leader of a cult, it may seem that the path he is following is one of awakening: perhaps through process of identification, perhaps through contiguous magic, analogous archetypal fragments in his own unconscious, so stimulated, will for the first time burst through their repressive barriers.

It should be obvious, then, that whatever the charismatic person, especially the leader of a cult, offers, it is not love, kindness, understanding, nurturance, empathy, or intimacy in any fundamental human sense. And if there is the promised enlightenment and guidance—whether religious, political, philosophical, moral, or aesthetic—you can be sure that it will be delivered grandiosely, and never in a personal way. It is no surprise that people upon first encountering a charismatic individual, especially in a one-on-one setting, soon realize that he can never be fulfilled with just one person, and that the relationship he is really looking for can be satisfied only by an audience: and collusively, in an effort to please, they often begin to respond in that way, as though they were members of an invisible but suggestible audience, an interaction that is rewarded and instantly reciprocated by their animated partner, who only then feels adequately appreciated.

We can sum up by saying that what the charismatic person exclusively wants is to institute a group process, and therefore feels compelled to convert ordinary interpersonal relationships to those of performing artist and audience (Alper, 1992).

THE SEDUCTIVE PERSONALITY

Since all charismatic people, in one way or another, seem to be seductive, while seductive people are not necessarily charismatic, it may be useful to distinguish between them.

In contrast to the more charismatic individual who usually prides himself on what I have called narcissistic honesty, the seductive personality relies upon sleight of hand, and one of the classic signs of a seduction attempt is its indirectness. There is always a hidden agenda, and even if it is initiated with the bold announcement "You're in love with me," a favorite ploy of Don Juans, the seducer on some level knows that everything he does is for effect.

To the extent that the relationship is predicated on securing control over the other person, it is based on power. The seductive person does not seem interested in relating for the sake of relating, in wanting to be with the other person in order to experience intimacy; rather, he is intent on gaining something private, narcissistic, and decidedly nonmutual. Seductiveness, in its compulsive covert machinations, implies that if what is desired were openly asked for, it would not be given. It follows that trickery and misdirection are tools of the trade. You can get what you want, provided you deceive the other person into thinking you want something else. Seductiveness, therefore, is almost always signified by a deep-rooted cynicism about human relating, and in the mind of the seducer appears this equation: Getting what he wants is synonymous with *corrupting* the other person.

Seductiveness may be characterized as the polar opposite of *nurturance*, which indicates hopefulness, the belief that if you are open, trusting, and giving, there is a real chance that instead of being exploited, your actions will be reciprocated. For similar reasons, seductive behavior is opposed to mutuality, and can be more suitably described as a contest, a game, or a zero-sum power struggle, in which there essentially can be only one winner and one loser. Since the seducer feels that he is taking what under normal circumstances would not be voluntarily given, he cannot help concluding that the person he has seduced has simply sold out. And by this curious logic, a seducer often will come to measure the magnitude of his seductive charm by assessing the extent to which he can corrupt another.

It is a mark of intimacy to be able to enjoy and sustain the flow of the process, without needing to hurry on to the end result. By contrast, the seductive person tends to view relating as an operational, externalized, step-by-step strategy, and relationships are accordingly judged on the merits of the particular strategy: i.e., a relationship that is failing = a person who is not being successfully seduced = a miscalculation or the application of the wrong strategy.

It is understandable, therefore, that the seductive personality will search for and tend to gauge potential partners in terms of their weakness, inferiority, and vulnerability to being exploited. It is not unfair to describe such a relationship as one of *predator and prey*, and the "right person" will often mean the right Achilles heel. It all follows from the fact that, since the seducer believes nothing will ever be given to him simply because he is valued for what he is, he must take what he wants. For such a person, a potential relationship can only mean a potential performance (i.e., work), and it is easy to see why the seducer, like the charismatic personality, feels a need to psych himself up. For such a person, who believes he is seeking what would never be voluntarily given, it seems natural that the performance that is given in exchange must be unusually potent. Not only that, given that the seducer is convinced beforehand he will meet resistance, the performance must also divert attention from its true aims.

In this sense, *seduction is a spell, and a seducer relates by trying to cast a spell.* Yet since he knows full well that the person to be seduced is far from hypnotized and always retains the power to say no, a fundamental strategy is to delay the moment of truth when the decision whether to be seduced or not will be made until the subject is in the most excited, and therefore most vulnerable, state. And this is where the art of casting a spell comes in. Everything is done to perpetuate the illusion that the intended victim is about to receive something both wonderful and utterly safe: that merely by walking down the proverbial garden path, only good things will arise, and that there is nothing to fear if one allows oneself to slip into the most relaxed, stimulated, and anticipatory state. At that precise moment, the true object of the seduction (e.g., sexual intercourse) is swiftly introduced, and whatever is necessary is done to coax, charm, coerce, and overcome the weakened defenses by boldly appealing to the aroused expectation elicited by the spell. If the seduction is consummated, it is often subsequently justified by pointing out that the person had every opportunity to say no but didn't, and really knew what the seducer was after but pretended not to know, so as to be absolved from responsibility, and therefore was just as devious as the perpetrator. After all, as the maxim goes, you can't cheat an honest man, so the seduced person all along must have wanted to be seduced—and in this fashion, the seducer rationalizes the seduction by implying that there was a tacit collusion of corrupt motives. It is no surprise that a favorite tactic is to begin by devaluing and demoralizing the person to be seduced, in the hope of creating a climate that will be conducive to corruption.

Here are some other standard strategies of the seducer (nonsexual as well as sexual):

- Flattery. This is the ultimate in interpersonal misdirection: to excite the victim's narcissism by a barrage of sweet talk, so as to deflect attention from the frank desire to exploit. Flattery is advance reparation of a sort for the corrupt act that the person to be seduced sooner or later will be asked to perform. It is nicely encapsulated in the classic joke, "I'll respect you in the morning." Flattery also implies that the seducer is doing what he is doing only because he is in awe of, and under the spell of, the other: in other words, he is *not* a seducer, he is just a harmless, lovesick admirer, who himself has been seduced into irresistibly praising the object of his affections.

- Light-heartedness, good-fellowship, wholeheartedness. Seducers love to deny the underlying sleaziness of their aims, and to defuse latent anxieties that corruption is in the air.

- Frank boasting of evil intentions. When ordinary seductiveness is fused with pathological sadism, the result can be a chilling, demonic persona. Thanks to a grandiose manic denial, there **is an** attempt to be narcissistically up front about what is to happen, with the attitude that there is no need to hide what is being planned, because the force of the evil seductive power is so overwhelming it will sweep everything before it. Finally, there is the sadistic pleasure that comes from informing the victim in advance of the fate in store.

- Seduction of values. Typically, seducers wish to repeat their **seductions**, despite their fondness for one-night stands. There is no better way than to foster a more corrupt view of life, in which one is amenable to being seduced in the future. When this tactic works, it is surprisingly successful and often the person who has been seduced will apply a reciprocal reasoning: "Well, I'm no longer innocent (i.e., my values have been sufficiently soiled so that I can no longer claim I did not compromise myself)—therefore I might as well go ahead and enjoy myself." It follows that seducers, to capitalize on this, will justify and portray themselves as liberators of their victim's repressed unconscious (one of the most common resistances on the part of patients to interpretations offered by their therapists, is this: "Is it really there (in my unconscious) or is he seductively corrupting me by putting it there with his interpretation?").

The greatest nonhuman seducer is a drug, because:

- It is harmless-looking (a pill).

- It works by a series of small, incremental steps. Even if the drug is relatively fast-acting, the negative (corrupting) side effects and aftereffects are always delayed.
- It induces incremental states of excitation and feeling good.
- It thereby defers the real decision as to whether the user has overindulged in and ingested what are actually chemical poisons until well after the chief benefits have been experienced. The well-known intransigent denial of the addictive person deflects the attention as effectively as the human seducer from what is really being done to the body.

From this point of view, it is a remarkable fact, and hardly a coincidence, that the paradigmatic unconscious strategy of the psychological seducer parallels in so many key ways the natural physiological process of corrupting the body with dosages of toxic drugs.

But what of the comparison with the charismatic personality, with which we began this section? We can reply that while all charismatic people are seductive the difference seems to be that the charismatic person is much more interested in seducing the group or audience. Yet there is a similarity too. Charisma, when it works, is a seduction that emulates in several important ways the pattern of the more commonplace and generally less theatrical seductive personality. In spite of the fact that charisma is predicated on grandiose openness (narcissistic honesty), there is also a considerable hidden agenda: the charismatic person falsely suggests that he is interested in the other, while in fact he is only interested in feeding his own grandiosity. This is denied (delayed) by a pretence that, since he is obviously revealing so much of himself by continuously projecting his personality outward, he must be doing this in the hope of getting to know the other. And once the would-be fan, admirer, or disciple embraces the charisma as something genuine, there often will ensue a magnetic bond of sorts between them, which is then experienced as a seduction: the person has been seduced by the charisma.

The differences, however, are those of time. A charismatic seduction, in the sense of the induction of a disciple into a cult or sect, can take months or years (there are no analogous one-night stand inductions into cults); and the inevitable period of subsequent disillusionment—the horrible awakening to the fact that one has compromised oneself by selling out to a cult or a charismatic leader—can only come after separation and extrication. By contrast, in sexual seduction, for example, it is much harder to hide what is being hidden (a nonplatonic relationship is what is being sought), and the carnal desires sooner or later must be exposed. This is also true in the case of the seductive salesperson who is pretending to be giving service instead of hungering for a sale: and in this instance, the distracted would-be customer has to wait no longer than the moment when the first attempt is made to "close" the sale before he comprehends the underlying, and now open, seductiveness.

In terms of game theory (Berne, 1964), it is easy to see that the sexual seducer is usually playing a fast game in which the resolution (seductive payoff or failure) will be speedily reached. By contrast, the charismatic leader of a cult—whose target, one might say, is the psyche and not the body—because the scope of his intended conquest is so much larger and more ambitious, is prepared, if necessary, to play out his hand over some of the best years of his life.

Freud (1933) once wrote that the first seducer is the mother, who with her ministrations to the child's bodily hygiene cannot help stimulating and arousing pleasurable sensations in the genitals. And R. D. Laing (1969), the British psychoanalyst, has alluded to a mystification process that can be induced in even very small children by pathological mothering, a process so powerful that in certain instances it may be truly said that a child has been placed under a lifelong spell cast by the mother.

If those are just some of the paradigmatic roots of seduction, then arising from them may be cultures, ethnic traditions, and contemporary mores—which may be society's way of seducing its members into feeling good enough about themselves to stay in step with the prevailing ethos; and in this sense the process of acculturalization is also a seduction.

THE PSYCHOLOGY
OF THE CULT LEADER

The charismatic leader of a cult is rich in denial. He denies that there is a connection between the idiosyncratic details of his preferred utopian world-view and the deficits and fantasies of his childhood; such certainly was the case with Tony Patrano, who for all his supposed philosophical brilliance never once saw the obvious link between his lifelong search for the origins of a pure Americanism and the fact that he was an adopted child who could not remember (and angrily did not want to remember) his biological parents. He denies—by constantly locating everything he does within the larger and more grandiose context of his vision—that underlying his behavior are unmistakable signs of obsessively self-serving narcissism, dependency, and addictiveness. An example is Tony Patrano sleeping with one girlfriend in the morning and another in the evening, and then, as though to deny there were anything selfish or superficial about such behavior, pontificating, "Great men need to be sexually satisfied."

It is part of the grandiose denial of the leader of a cult to deny the existence of a personal unconscious. This means that whatever the leader does, it will somehow transcend a merely personal relationship; and if there is to be frank libido and aggression, then they are in the service of a collective archetype—which is why, philosophically, most cult leaders tend to be closer to Jung than to Freud.

For all these reasons, cult leaders may be said to suffer from a pathology of symbolism: they see themselves, literally, as symbols incarnate, and they symbolize everything about themselves. Analogous to schizophrenics, whose loosened associations engender an abnormal spread of meaning, such leaders are prone to a pathological spread of cult symbolism: e.g., as Tony Patrano once said to Matthew, "I really thought that this room, this chair, this sofa, everything about me, would one day be famous."

For a denial this powerful, there must be a suitable mechanism of defense, and it is easy to see, given their charismatic personality, that projection and projective identification will be called into play. And it is because of this mechanism that the leader of a cult can majestically deny even a scintilla of neurotic conflict, and, by projecting it onto society's deficits, externalize an unbearable inner tension into a paranoid them-against-us mentality.

There is still much that follows from such denial. Because their grandiosity is usually so pathological as to be fairly described as megalomania, what is called the narcissism of small differences, especially the idea of pettiness, is anathema to them. While they frequently admit they have failings, these are never petty but always tragic ones (the Achilles heel of the great man).

The leader of a cult tends to see himself as a great rebel, a messenger of a cultural salvation, and a kind of messianic genius (Bion, 1974). His genius as he sees it, has little to do with intelligence or intellectual attainment, but refers to the mystical power to comprehend, seize upon, and bring to birth a dormant but pregnant historical trend. Rules do not apply to such a man—or rather, existing rules, which he tends to see as toxic and persecutory restraints, and regards as part of his mission to overthrow. In their place, he will single-handedly usher in new rules and a new order of things.

Regarding the present body of laws and legal sanctions, therefore, the leader of a cult will see himself as a revolutionary protester and a founding father of a sorely needed and predestined new order. His compulsion to symbolize will lead him retrospectively to discern symbols pointing to his coming, and then feverishly to check for latent omens in contemporary, often popular, culture that augur that the tide is turning his way.

Because of his pathological possessiveness, the leader of a cult can view each desirable member as fair sexual game, and for Tony Patrano, who absolutely needed to think of himself as a great lover, it was a matter of honor to do his best to sleep with all female members (as he often told Matthew, "I think every woman is in love with me").

It is hardly adequate to say that the leader is in a symbiotic relationship with the members of the cult. Instead, he sees them as surrogate family members who must compensate him for everything his real family did not give him, and he therefore constitutes the cult so as to supply retrospective revenge and the undoing of genuine or fantasized damage done to him by his family of origin. Conversely, disciples are pathologically in search of a new family, and the ties between the cult and the member are just as often the expression of a collusive attempt magically to constitute a second family.

Unlike other charismatic figures, cult leaders are not expected to back up what they say, in the sense of coming out the winner in any immediate confrontation. Since they often command only a handful of followers, yet typically oppose themselves to the mainstream culture or political framework, they are generally bucking odds of over a million to one. By contrast, Muhammad Ali, the most charismatic figure of my youth, despite boasting loudly and often that he was the greatest, in order to back up his claim, had only to defeat one opponent at a time. And since he was easily the best prizefighter in the world in his prime, it was not only conceivable that he would, it was extremely probable. Yet the cult leader has to conquer not only millions of unbelievers, but often as well, hundreds, sometimes thousands of years of tradition. Victory, for a cult leader, understandably will be measured, instead, in symbols, portents, indicators, or undercurrents of Messianic reform, and is not quantified in a zero-sum way, in which somebody wins and somebody loses.

Unfortunately, for the psychology of cult leaders, all this accomplishes is to feed their grandiosity by removing them further and further from reality and reality-testing. After all, if nothing they do is going to be measured along normative lines constrained by social feedback—if, for example, a disciple can commit suicide by setting fire to himself, and later be adjudged to have performed a positive and heroic act by making a necessary cult statement—then anything and everything is possible. If the world as we presently know it is subject at any moment to a futuristic symbolic revision, and if all of the symbols to be used are the exclusive domain of the leader (a grotesque travesty of which was witnessed during the manic attack of Tony Patrano in Los Angeles), then the cult leader can become in his ability to juggle and reinterpret symbols at will, a pathological revisionist of reality.

It may be instructive to look at a man who, though phenomenally charismatic, was sane—and to note the differences. Muhammad Ali (Hauser, 1991) was a member of a sect, the Black Muslims, which promised to liberate blacks from the white devils and pave the way for an eventual takeover by avenging blacks, who were biding their time in a spaceship located high above the earth. Yet Ali, although he was a devout believer, was wise enough to leave the leading and the prophesying in the Black Muslims to others (and with it the responsibility for backing it up), and to enjoy a controversial but protected status as a celebrated follower. It was a manifestation of his being in touch with the limits of his personality, and the fact that, unlike every cult leader, he knew the boundaries of his charisma. It is part of the reason he has not only survived but has become a folk hero.

So potent and persuasive is the seductive power of cults and cult leaders that on occasion it has been likened to brainwashing. Yet the association with the terror and force used to brainwash POWs is tenuous at best. Most cults do not come close to equaling the absolute physical control of their members that can be achieved in prisons and concentration camps. Accordingly, the indoctrination tactics are vastly more psychological. In a cult, the main threat seems to be, in one form or another, expulsion. When it is appreciated, however, that the cult, to the fully initiated member like Matthew, is much more binding than even a pathologically dysfunctional and symbiotic family, that instead of being just one family among millions of families on earth it is conceived of as the family, or the family as universe—then banishment from the cult can seem like banishment from the world.

Although the psychological leverage this confers is enormous and cannot be overestimated, it is nevertheless not brainwashing, because that term seems to imply that what happens when a person becomes intensively indoctrinated somehow entails a manipulation or alteration of his brain. It is therefore significant that the brain and not the mind is implicated, and it reflects the American denial that the instances of so-called "brainwashing" alleged to occur periodically in this country can possibly be examples, as I believe they usually are, even when physical abuse is involved, of an essentially psychological process. Such denial reached its pinnacle in the insistence on seeing Patti Hearst—despite the fact that she had been abducted and tortured by an obviously psychotic sect—as completely and legally responsible for her subsequent actions; as though there is a time limit for how long it is permissible to be broken in spirit and no longer yourself, after having been systematically terrorized, before you are expected to snap out of it and pull your weight once again as a law-abiding citizen.

In the cult, the psychological equivalent of "brainwashing" seems to occur in a fairly orderly sequence of steps. First, there is the concentrated seduction and indoctrination of the potentially new member. Almost simultaneously, there is a universal devaluation of everything in the world outside the cult: society, friends, parents, teachers, culture, religion. Concomitantly, there is a continuous attempt to supply substitute gratifications for what one has been asked to reject in the normal world: new philosophical teachings, pleasure, socializing, sexual partners, creative outlets, a system of reward and recognition—all are offered, and are supposed now to come only from the inner world of the cult. When this has taken hold in the mind of the disciple, he is hooked, and the ultimate threat, expulsion, will be as devastating to him as enforced physical withdrawal is to the drug addict.

An important part of this process, which greatly reinforces it, is the rites of passage. At a certain point the disciple will be asked to provide proof of commitment by performing a difficult service, or symbolically displaying unequivocal allegiance to the cult (e.g., shaving the head, publicly distributing proselytizing leaflets, or, as in Matthew's case, participating in an assault on the college lecture circuit). On one level, such a rite of passage is meant to represent, in the mind of the disciple, a kind of burning of bridges. On another level, in the mind of the leader of the cult, it is perhaps a test of unconditional love: Will you never abandon me no matter what I demand of you?

The final stage is reached when the disciple has passed the tests and is considered addicted. Demands are then escalated, greater and greater control is sought, until the depleted and by now psychically incapacitated member, who could not continue even if he wanted to, is forced to leave. Psychologically, to continue the drug addiction analogy, this is equivalent to bottoming out of the cult.

To sum up: What the cult leader finds unbearable and cannot accept is what is apparent to most sensitive observers who encounter but are not influenced by him—that he is hungry for love and recognition, desperate and insecure, and nearly completely dependent upon the admiration of others.

Aftermath of a Manic-Depressive Attack

One became a drug addict. One became a drug dealer. One spent a month in jail. Families were disrupted, and lives were put on hold. All spent years wallowing, in various degrees, in the depression and demoralization that are sure to come in the wake of a manic-depressive attack; and when the patient happens to be someone who calls himself Tony Thunder—who in the face of all logic boldly lives out his psychotic fantasies while still managing to hold onto the reins of power—the effect is catastrophic.

For someone like Matthew swept up in its center, such a manic-depressive attack can seem even more chaotic and threatening than a war zone. And coming out of it can seem like returning from a battlefront or coming down from a cocaine binge. There is an inevitable period of rather extensive crashing. The discrepancy between the high-octane life of a manic phase and the subsequent banality of everyday real life is so glaring as to seem unreal, and the initial reaction is often one of depressive denial—e.g., Matthew's disbelief, upon being ordered to grind out his cigarette by an imperious flight attendant, that such pettiness could possibly be inflicted upon him.

There is a sense, upon returning to the real world, that what has really happened is that one has been swindled. This is because the manic attack, with its onslaught of dynamic optimism, seems to be saying that right around the corner lies something good and magical and—although it is in the nature of a manic attack, because of its psychotic organization, that nothing ever goes as planned—it can thereby effectively create an us-against-them wartime hope that eventually the battle will be won. Those such as Matthew, who blindly follow a manic leader who is traveling through a living hell, need to sustain themselves with a desperate belief that somehow they will emerge victorious at the end. And when the end does come, usually in total shambles, with everything lost, there is necessarily bitter disillusionment and a clear retrospective verdict that one was simply seduced by a manic attack.

It was the most difficult pill to swallow, and it contributed in no small part to Matthew's conclusion that he had been unmercifully manipulated. But there is much more than disenchantment, self-flagellation, and recrimination. There is identity diffusion and identity crisis. For a manic attack of such symbiotic magnitude as Tony Thunder's can actually electrify the fragmented psyches of its teetering disciples, and, through unremitting hyperstimulation and nonstop drama, provide pseudo-cohesiveness. The feeling of being incorporated into the psychical force field of an extended manic attack is like having a nightmare—it is incoherent, yes, but also unforgettable in its riveting mounting horror, and a person so caught up in it is easily spellbound and cannot look away. It is almost as though the surcharge of drama and overstimulation completely distract the disciple from what under any other circumstances would produce catastrophic anxiety: that his ego, like everything else around him, is also crumbling.

RECOVERY AND REENTRY

Recovery does not come from deprogramming or desensitizing. That is a denial of the fact that the central conflict of the initiated member long preceded the actual induction into the cult. The idea of deprogramming, seen in this light, is only a behavioral externalization and projection of an inner psychical readiness to be indoctrinated onto the evil persona of a master manipulator. And the same may be said of its behavioral counterproposal: a "good" deprogrammer is meant to be a comparably effective manipulator, who happens to be working on the right side.

This idea robs the recovering cult member of responsibility. Recovery, instead, comes with the recognition and acceptance of the antecedent state or even the hunger to be converted to some kind of substitute family. It is necessary therefore to explore past relationships with his real family, to see the connection between this family and the cult family, to understand in depth the diabolical dynamics of cult addiction, and to link it retrospectively to the original family deprivation that must have preceded it. The recovering cult member needs to reclaim or perhaps start anew a developmental journey that traumatically, for one reason or another, was significantly arrested, and not only by the cult.

Such a process of recovery will be marked by sadness, acceptance, and ultimately forgiveness for the undeniable fact that the true believer committed a colossal and near-fatal blunder in his choice of a role model.

It has to be understood that while the substitute cult activities constituted a detour in personal development—given the deprivation that preceded it—they were nevertheless inevitable.

The developmental panic at becoming truly autonomous and the issue of identity diffusion, which generally precede the induction into a cult, must be examined in depth.

A recovering member of a cult is like a recovering alcoholic, and must learn to live without the "high" of the cult's charisma and be weaned away from such pseudo-identity thrills.

There is the issue of survivor's guilt. When a cult catastrophically collapses, as the Cult of the Frontiersmen did in Los Angeles, and the leader goes down in the flames of madness, as Tony Thunder did, it is difficult to believe that one will not somehow be punished for not having joined him—and that one's survival is really an abandonment, an act of disloyalty.

There is also the issue of the survivor's dependency needs. Once one has been successfully weaned away from the numerous symbiotic gratifications doled out by the cult, the underlying dependency needs, which are enormous, can be expected to surface, and must be dealt with.

Psychotherapy can be helpful, because unlike with other addictions, there are few (if any) cult-recovery peer groups, and by the nature of cult bottoming out, surviving members tend to disperse and not come together into support groups. Accordingly, there is no real framework in America within which to acknowledge the battered survivors of cult indoctrination, as there are for other kinds of victims: Holocaust, crime, incest, drug abuse, and so forth.

Because of this lack of a support network, the victims of cults often react negatively to their fellow survivors, and instead of finding the comfort they need, they tend to see one another as punitive reminders of a shared trauma. They often shun each other's company, and it is not uncommon that following the collapse of a cult, those who had been brothers and sisters in symbiosis became thereafter strangers for life.

A month or so after Matthew had concluded the story of his induction, escape, and return, he removed a small figure from his wallet and showed it to me. About three inches high, made of cotton, felt, and string, with a red cape on its back, and a blue shirt front with an "S" on the chest, it was a doll sewn by his mother at his insistent request when he was seven, and it represented his great hero from the comics, Superman. Racing around the house, holding the Superman doll extended in his fist, he had tried to kindle in himself the same exhilarating sense of superhuman, gravity-defying power he imagined his hero to have.

Then one day he decided to turn his fantasy into reality, and at the same time to test what he already considered the dubious existence of God. So, although he never said his bedtime prayers, he spoke this prayer: *Let me wake up in the morning, just once, and fly around the ceiling of my room like Superman.*

It was a brilliant pact, which in one stroke would prove the existence of God, and, even more crucial, of God's love for him. Yet such was the extent of his demoralization and his lack of faith, although he was still only seven years old, that as soon as his feet hit the cold floor on the morning of what was to be the day of his great flight, he did not even bother to see if he could elevate. He just knew that he could not, and that there could not be a God who would love him enough to grant even a fleeting taste of superhuman power.

Matthew smiled at the simple but profound connection between his hopelessness, his yearning to be a superman, and his later spellbound reaction to the only person he would ever encounter who had professed to have, and be able to give, superhuman power.

It was his first genuine insight into what must have preceded by many years his indoctrination into the Cult of the Frontiersmen—and at that moment, it could be said, his real therapy began.

PART II

THE BOILER ROOM

HUNTING FOR MEN

"It was amazing. No matter what I said, no matter what anyone said, he had the answer. He was like a *robot*!"

Spoken with affection and admiration, this was meant to convey some of the pleasure Paul had felt upon encountering his first genuine super-salesman, Ralph Cavalere, the district manager from Westchester, who had unexpectedly dropped into the newly opened office, a rectangular, underfurnished space located in mid-Manhattan, and was going to show the resident trainees how it was done.

And the name of the game when it came to selling was called "overcoming objections." From the standpoint of making and closing a sale, an objection was defined as anything and anyone that stood in your way, and as Paul was soon to learn, for the expert salesman there was no such thing as an objection that could not be overcome.

The hard part, however, the part that took months, sometimes years, to acquire, which separated the neophyte from the ace, was the ingenuity, perseverance, motivation to succeed, refusal to be discouraged that together, almost magically it seemed, could transform the most diehard No into a cash-register-ringing Yes.

To demonstrate such state-of-the-art sales prestidigitation, Ralph Cavalere (the robot) had planted himself in the center of the room flanked by Paul, Cindy, and Arthur (the rookies), and had invited the toughest, most unanswerable, ego-crushing, sales-killing objections that they had encountered, or could imagine encountering. The product they were being trained to sell, by cold-calling on the telephone, happened to be typewriter supplies, but it could as easily have been encyclopedias, Florida land deals, mutual funds, or box seats in the opera, because the product was unimportant (only losers needed the crutch of believing in what they sold), while the true salesman relied solely on himself, his guile, and above all, his killer instinct.

It was the killer instinct, the ruthlessness when it came to undermining even the most heartfelt objection, that so impressed Paul, and eager to test whether such a pose of invincibility could possibly be real, he was glad to contribute what he considered his most forceful objections.

"I'm overstocked as it is."

"What I have in mind is supplies that you'll need when you run out."

"That will be in about six months. Call me back then."

"I'd be happy to. Meanwhile, what I could do for you now is place an order, specifying that you won't be filling it until a certain date."

"But then you'd be earning interest on my money. I'd rather do that for myself."

"You could defer the bulk of the payment and only put down the minimum deposit, if you like. But if you wait for six months, the increase in prices that is coming will more than offset any benefits you derive from savings on interest. And besides, most people don't take money out of the bank to buy these supplies; they use money they were going to spend anyway."

"How can I trust a stranger on the telephone?"

"You're not being asked to. Everything will be specified in writing, and if you're not perfectly satisfied, you can cancel the order up to seventy-two hours afterward, and there'll be no penalty."

"I've heard of people getting tricked by fine print."

"There's no fine print in the confirmation of our order. You'll see that for yourself. But if it'll make you feel better, I'll send you a list of names of some of our satisfied customers, whom you could check with."

"I've never done business with strangers in my life."

"But weren't all the people you now trust the most once

strangers to you? Isn't what's important not how long you know someone but how well someone performs for you? But since this is the first time, instead of the regular order of one hundred gross, why don't you start with just the small order of thirty gross?"

"This sounds like a sales pitch to me."

"It is if I don't deliver the goods, but if you give me the opportunity, I'll prove to you, at no risk whatsoever, that it's an excellent business offer."

"I want to see something in writing first. Send me a brochure."

"Is your address _____? I'll get that right out to you. Meanwhile, I can answer some of the questions I'm sure you'll have right now, while we're speaking on the telephone."

"Tell me, do you get a commission if I buy?"

"Not the first time. But if you reorder, I get a small bonus, and that's my incentive to make sure that you're a satisfied customer."

"You sound like a con man to me."

"It's natural to be suspicious of someone who calls you on the telephone, but the fact is that ninety percent of American business is conducted by two people just talking on the telephone; and what's more, according to the Better Business Bureau, the ethical standards of telephone salesmen are higher than those in any other branch of business."

Paul was happy to stop here, assured that he had found out what he wanted to know. If he had had the courage to say, in the spirit of the ultimate devil's advocate, something purely outrageous, such as "Fuck you," or even threatening, such as "If you don't get off the phone, I'll come down there and beat the shit out of you"—he was certain that Ralph Cavalere, sitting there almost lazily with his arms folded across his chest, would have regarded it as just one more objection to be swatted down.

In the six weeks that he worked for Barstar Enterprises, before it folded up like so many boiler rooms before and after it, Paul received a crash course in what it takes to become a star high-pressure salesman. He learned that it was not enough to be able to ad-lib lies on the spot, one had to lie believably, as Ralph

Cavalere (the best, because the most realistic, liar he had ever met) loved to demonstrate. He learned that high-pressure sales, especially telephone sales, are founded on the quick takedown, the one-shot score, the kill; that its bible is the "pitch," usually a short presentation that turns on a selling hook or gimmick believed to be especially powerful, persuasive, and above all, deceptive.

In the case of Barstar Enterprises, the hook (the nuts and bolts of the pitch for selling typewriter supplies) hinged on the word "gross," meaning a dozen dozen, and the incidental but crucial fact that the average buyer did not know the meaning of the word and was therefore easily led into thinking that a purchase of, say, five gross boxes of typewriter ribbons meant something like five dozen boxes. And generally it was not until the buyer received a shipment approximately twelve times the size of the one he thought he had ordered, long past the time when it was legally possible to cancel or reduce the order, did he realize how badly he had been duped.

It never failed to astonish Paul, who was sensitive and intelligent, not only how well such bald and simplistic selling hooks worked, but the apparent reverence in which they were held by even master salesmen such as Ralph Cavalere, who, upon being informed by Paul, at his hiring, just how measly he considered the pitch, had sincerely replied, "Look, it's been around for thirty years, so it must have something."

Yet, indispensable though the pitch was, it was the quality of the salesmanship with which it was delivered that made the difference; and in order to verify this, one had only to witness and compare the identical presentation being read, first, by novices like Cindy, Arthur, and himself, and then by a veteran like Ralph Cavalere.

In spite of his admiration, Paul knew that his own strengths lay elsewhere—in his soft-spokenness, his nice-guy demeanor that led people immediately to trust him, and his understated but extraordinary single-mindedness—and not in the brazen antisocial stance of a Ralph Cavalere, who expressed flat-out contempt for customers ("marks") and rival salesmen ("losers"); who displayed more interest in the brand names and merits of items of apparel, wristwatches, or neckties he had recently acquired than in his relations with his associates; and who enjoyed reminiscing about his days as a Green Beret in the Vietnam jungles, when it was possible, if you were a cold-eyed appraiser of men's strengths and weaknesses, as he was, to tell within twenty-four hours "who was going to make it, and who wasn't."

Paul learned other things: that for dyed-in-the-wool high-pressure salesmen, selling was an interminable process—it began the moment you met other salesmen and it was there when you worked with them, drank with them, went looking for women with them, argued with them, competed with them. Until you realized that it was their one and indispensable way of relating not only to each other but to the world, and for them literally everything—sex, love, money, power, self-image—came down to whether they made, or did not make, the sale.

Paul remembered his surprise upon first encountering such a biased mindset: when a frantic young telephone salesman, nicknamed "the Flasher" because of his fondness for wearing gaudy polyester suits, upon discussing the Vietnam debacle had solemnly opined, "If we'd had salesmen out there to present our cause instead of generals, we would have won that war." And while he could deal with such cases of distorted self-praise by laughing at them, he was unable to do so with Ralph Cavalere, who one day, matter-of-factly, told him about his favorite Vietnam war buddy, José, and his passion for hunting.

"You mean hunting for animals in the jungle?" asked Paul innocently.

"Hunting for men. He liked to fly solo night raids and drop napalm on tiny villages."

It was not lost on Paul that he was different from such men, but that did not mean that he could not, in due course, successfully compete, especially if he did so on his own terms, playing from his strength: so where they were devious and slick, he would be believable, where they were agile and ingenious, he would be solid, and where they were opportunistic and aggressive, he would be patient and determined.

In the four years since he had graduated from City College with a major in business, which pointed him nowhere, those assets had worked well enough to land him any sales job he applied for, but were unable to help him thereafter. For reasons he had not quite figured out, despite his best efforts, none of the promises made to him, nor the hopes he had fostered, ever materialized.

It was part of Paul's stubbornness to insist, right up until the day I met him, that his continual failure had nothing to do with the fact that he admittedly did not have what is called a sales personality, but was simply the result of having chosen the wrong companies. So long as he did not allow himself to be discouraged, it would only be a matter of time before he would find the right company, the right product, and would make his mark.

And the right product for Paul, unlike Ralph Cavalere, was one he could believe in; what was more, he prided himself on this difference in temperaments, that he was honest and dependable, someone who elected to run his life according to consciously cultivated principles, and was not sleazy like the others. So he did not let it bother him that they considered him a square and a good Samaritan; that they laughed when he told them how, seeing a purse snatcher, he had chased him for a good three blocks; and how, when he had had his wallet professionally picked—one man knocking him to the ground, another lifting his wallet, and a third blocking his way so that he could not pursue the thief—he had furiously broken free and would have run a mile, if that was what it took, to apprehend the pickpocket.

Injustices such as this, clearcut violations of another person's rights, flagrant breaches of promise, typically infuriated Paul, and he considered it a point of honor to do all he could to redress them. He liked this part of himself, and if the men and the women he worked with were considerably less than honorable, it made him feel that much better about himself. There were other parts of himself that he thought highly of. And when you came

right down to it, he did not think it hyperbole to say that he possessed an admirably well-rounded personality: he was intelligent,
decidedly more so than the average salesman (whom he enjoyed
intimidating with his knowledge of computers and finance); he
could ski; he could box; he worked out regularly in a nearby
health club and had an excellent build; he was a completely confident, adaptable traveler who was unafraid to visit any part of the
world; he was absolutely trustworthy when it came to his closest
friends, who invariably stayed loyal to him; and he was a devoted
son who never failed to do what he could to make life simpler,
smoother, and sweeter for his aging, doting parents.

If he had one weakness, it was his gullibility, his inability to
accept that people not only might not like or respect him, but
actually might wish to exploit him—and it was on such gullibility
that he subsequently laid the blame for his miserable string of
choices when it came to prospective employers.

His initial choice, and fiasco, soon after he graduated from
City College, was a small company called Rover Books, Inc., situated in a lower-East-Side office, which pretended to be modeled
after the famous Time-Life Book subscription series, but in
essence was a telephone sales boiler-room operation.

Along with about twenty other trainees, sitting in rows of geo-
metrically aligned matching aluminum desks, each sporting a
telephone, a telephone directory, and a small handbell, to be
rung by a blow of the palm, Paul was given a single sheet of typed
instructions on how to sell the featured monthly books to random customers who most likely had never purchased a book
through the mail before. It was therefore designated "cold-calling," and the sheet of typewritten instructions was the "pitch," but
because it was a noncommissioned, and therefore a "low-pressure," sale, it was a relatively innocuous delivery: just a recital of
the alleged product benefits, hopefully in a dynamically interesting and believable voice, plus the close, which was the standard
"If you're not totally satisfied with the book of your choice after
ten days, just send it back and there will be no charge." And the
books that were offered—in the hope of appealing to the widest

possible range of customers—were usually how-to (e.g., how to be your own carpenter or electrician), standbys such as chronicles of the Civil War, lives of the American Presidents, turning points of the twentieth century, great generals throughout history.

It was all so cut and dried, so simple as pie. How could he not succeed? Only if it were not a fair deal, if the cards were somehow stacked against him, if the rosy picture that had been painted of how easy it was to make sales, of the money and bonuses that would effortlessly accrue, were a shameless come-on.

He would not believe that, and judging by that first exciting day, he had been lucky, and right, and wise in his choice of jobs. For what could have been more fun than the way they all lined up and poised themselves expectantly on the brink of their unrelieved five-hour shift of telephoning, and at the crack of nine, like thoroughbreds shooting out of the starting gate, reached for their telephones? To dial nonstop (going to the bathroom seemed unproductive, and was generally postponed), using the Watts line to gain access to nearly any household in America, repeating the pitch so many times that you memorized it in a day, all the while keeping an eye, breathlessly, on the finish line, to see who would win. Winning meant tallying the most number of sales in the room, and it brought with it a cash bonus, bragging rights for the day, plus a small prize (such as a toaster or an alarm clock).

At the end of that first five-hour shift, after driving himself mercilessly, Paul had accounted for the sale of ten books, and he had come in second to the winner, who had sold thirteen. Both of them had fallen far short of the twenty sales, that were required to be eligible for the major incentive, a fifty-percent increase in the hourly rate (which was minimum), and you did not have to be a math whiz to realize that the incentive had been deliberately set high enough so as to be unattainable by even a super-salesman.

Because the tempo and pace are so accelerated in a boiler room, it is easy to learn—but the lessons that are learned are overwhelmingly negative. Paul realized that regardless of whether the actual pitch was a bland soft sell, as with Rover Books, there was no such thing as low pressure in a boiler room, especially when it came to the working conditions. Extraordinary force was directed, and great attention was paid, to how to milk absolutely the last drop of work from the exhausted bodies of employees. Nothing, therefore, could be left to chance, and Paul was to learn that whatever happened, it was usually for a reason. Thus, the constant revolving door of trainees meant that the energy level required to function under such stress was rapidly depleted, and it was necessary continually to bring in fresh troops. If there were silly things like handbells on each desk to be struck at the conclusion of each sale, that was because it had been discovered that the promotion and reinforcement of competition among sales personnel would enhance performance. And if there were a steady barrage of belittling, verbal whipping, and shaming from the sales manager, Allan Hauseman, and occasionally, when morale was really low, the branch manager himself, John Gable—well, that was because it had been demonstrated that when a person is demoralized and hopeless and beyond self-motivation,it is incumbent upon the leader to goad and spur that person by whatever means possible.

None of this was lost on Paul, who was a quicker study than most, but whose undoing came precisely when it dawned on him that they were attempting to control him totally, because that was when his stubbornness kicked in. As long as he was there, until he could find another job, he would not let them do that.

But it was easier said than done: Paul discovered, like others before him, that his first day would be his best, because it would take no longer than that to realize that no matter how extraordinarily hard he worked, there would be no payoff whatever. And since it was pointless to try to excel, there was no other alternative but to try to conserve one's energy and survive: which meant to establish the average sales per person in the room (about four), and gauge one's efforts accordingly.

For about two months, then, Paul jealously monitored his output, and while he never went over ten sales, he often came perilously close to dropping below four. He was to learn that once your heart was no longer in it, to deliver even the minimum in a telephone sales boiler room becomes increasingly and excruciatingly difficult.

So he was no longer puzzled that the turnover rate was so remarkably high: he saw that the majority of incoming sales trainees, who did not have his toughness or determination, would be forced to quit if they were not fired first. He could sense, although he could not hear, the badgering and the latent threats that took place behind closed doors whenever Allan Hauseman found it necessary to closet himself with a consistently low-producing trainee.

He noticed that sometimes after such reprimands, the underachiever in question, even though it was early in the shift, would summarily head home, as though expelled from school; and he wondered whether in addition to that humiliation, the further penalty of a day's loss of pay had been tacked on.

That was something he would not let them do. Nor would he let anyone talk down to him directly, disparage him in any gross fashion, or infringe upon any of his rights, which were precious few.

And for two months, as long as he maintained his average of at least four sales a day, no one did. Then one week, drained and infuriated at still having to repeat word for word the identical pitch, that he had already recited thousands of times, without exactly being aware of it, or not wanting to be aware, he allowed his sales to dip to an average of about two and a half per day.

When Allan Hauseman invited him into his office for their first-closed-door chat, Paul had come to his senses and was ready to turn over a new leaf and to return at least to his minimum of four Rover Book sales a day. He was not worried, therefore, about the outcome of their conversation, but he was more than curious as to whether the degree of respect with which the anticipated reprimand was to be delivered would meet his standards.

Until then Hauseman had behaved as though he were Paul's friend, as he behaved toward everyone in the room, up to the time when he considered it expedient to fire them. He was a short, over-weight, dynamic twenty-year-old reported to have "a mind like a computer," rumored to have rebelled against his Episcopalian-minister father in Philadelphia and to be living a wildly profligate life in the fast lane in Manhattan, and when he wasn't talking sales, he liked to make what he considered smart repartee.

There was little repartee as Hauseman, his hands officiously folded on top of his imposing but bare desk, briefly reviewed Paul's performance over the preceding two months. Initially it had been very good, and there had been hope that one day Paul might even ascend to the level of assistant manager, which would have greatly pleased him. After all, as he was certain Paul surely knew, he liked him, was well aware that he was a nice guy, sensitive, gentle, loyal, and determined, with, of course, the potential to be a star salesman. But of late, no, for at least a month, Paul's performance had mysteriously eroded and was steadily slipping. Gone were the snap and the charisma, the refusal to take no for an answer, and in their place was a kind of depressed, hangdog attitude that seemed very unlike him.

As though satisfied that he had now displayed the required comraderie, empathy, and nurturance, Hauseman, drew himself up in his chair. It was time to get down to the bottom line of a bottom-line business: which was that four sales a day over the past month was nothing to write home about, and two and a half sales a day over the past week was positively disgusting. Was Paul trying to take advantage of the well-known good nature of Allan Hauseman? And if he was, did he now realize how sadly mistaken he had been? To slam home the point that only top-drawer performance would ever be acceptable at Rover Books, Hauseman hunched forward and said, "So go home, Paul, and think it over. And as for your rotten showing the past month ... fuck you!"

For a second, Paul had to struggle with his original reaction, which was to punch Allan Hauseman in the center of his round complacent face, or at least grab him by the shirt front. What he settled for was to get up from his chair furiously and position his forefinger about an inch from his sales manager's chest.

"I'm *staying*, Allan. And don't you ... ever ... ever ... ever talk to me like that again."

And stay Paul did, spitefully selling fewer books than ever (one), but continually trying to stare Hauseman down, conveying the violent message that the only way to get rid of him would be either by fighting him or having the police escort him out of the office.

Heartened by his bold and successful defiance of his sales manager, he no longer cared that his sales steadily dropped: and when John Gable, in one of his infrequent pep talks delivered to the entire room, had concluded, "So now that I've made a clown out of myself by entertaining you, why don't you clowns get back on the telephone and show me what you can do," Paul had quietly raised his hand.

"I'm not a clown."

"What?"

"I said I'm not a clown."

"You're not?"

"Right. I'm not."

He thought he was ready to defend himself in whatever way necessary when two days later, the branch manager, from behind his desk, which was behind the plate-glass window, simply wagged his finger at him. Paul told himself, as he headed for the office and an inevitable dressing down, that while he would not be rude, neither would he tolerate abuse. In a straightforward way, he would unburden himself, explaining that the recent decline in his sales and his uncharacteristically aggressive behavior were both products of the low morale in the room, which in turn had been created by the abominable working conditions.

What Paul did not realize was that there were few things in the world John Gable was less interested in than being an audience to a subordinate salesman's discontents. He was a stocky tough guy with red hair and a baseball announcer's gravelly voice, whose favorite motto was, "I eat determination for lunch," and he liked to pepper his impromptu motivational talks with vignettes culled from his days as a teenage driver of an ice-cream truck in New

Jersey. The underlying moral was plain enough: if you really want something, there are no nos, only yeses, even if you sometimes have to grab them by the throat.

And apparently, judging by his performance of late, Paul had become a large no in the mind of John Gable. So leaning across the desk, in his man-to-man style, he said, "Look, I'm having a problem with you."

"I can explain why my figures are dropping. I think ..."

"I really don't give a shit what you think."

Four years later, Paul would remember how a single brief sentence had wiped away two months of resistance.

"He meant it, and there was nothing I could say to that. Somehow I thought I was involved in a silent battle with the company, and while I knew he didn't like me, I wanted to believe that he respected me. But when I saw that he didn't, that there was absolutely no relationship of any kind between us, I suddenly felt like a slave."

He would be a slave no more. Collecting his paycheck, he headed two blocks north to a company called Pernell, Inc. (specializing in office supplies) and the opportunity to make, as they were fond of saying, big bucks. With money would come power, and with power, freedom: the right to determine his own future.

It was all predicated, once again, on the pitch. It was the pitch that had been perfected over a decade and had withstood the test of time as effectively as the Twelve Steps of Alcoholics Anonymous; that had secured for Sid Pernell and his wife a palatial house in the Five Towns in Long Island, and could earn for his salespeople—if they listened to what he told them and did exactly as he said—up to one thousand dollars a week.

What was the sales pitch? Essentially this:

"Are you Mr. (Ms.) _____ of _____ Company? Yes? Then congratulations! You have just won a week's paid vacation in Florida!"

Much of the mandatory intensive two-day sales training program consisted in learning to deliver the opening lines with the desired blend of contagious enthusiasm and professional credibility. It was considered crucial that the buyer believe he actually had won a free vacation, because the entire pitch depended on deflecting attention away from the order (with its excessively high prices) that had to be purchased to be eligible to collect the prize. When Paul innocently inquired as to whether free vacations were really given to customers who bought office supplies, he was candidly told that yes, they were, but that only two percent opted to receive their prize. That was because the site of the paid vacation was a tiny motel located in the hinterlands of Florida, and since airfare was not included, the majority of "winners," on thinking it through, soon realized that they had won nothing.

It was Paul's first introduction to the questionable borderline sales practices beloved by high-pressure salesmen, not exactly illegal unless flagrantly abused, not exactly a scam, but that—in spite of the aggressive contempt they show for the ethics of business transactions—are, surprisingly, tolerated. And while he had already learned from his experience at Rover Books that the first sale that is made in a boiler room is the one that sells the job to the incoming trainee, he nevertheless cautiously hoped that he would be able, if he tried his absolute best, to salvage at least a respectable percentage of the one-thousand-dollars-a-week carrot that had been waved in his face.

So, for a week straight, scarcely straying from his assigned cubicle, Paul tried every conceivable permutation of voice, tone, excitement level, and believability so as to deliver most effectively the magical sentence "Congratulations! You have just won a week's paid vacation in Florida," and then deal, if he had to, with the objections (which were mostly of the I-don't-believe-you variety). Given how incredibly hard he had worked, it was no surprise that at the end of the first week he led the room in sales, but he could not mask his disappointment that he had only earned three hundred and thirty dollars. Since Paul's draw (which had to be paid back) the first two months was three hundred and fifty dollars a week, it meant he was already twenty dollars in arrears.

At the end of that first week, Sid Pernell invited Paul into his office for a friendly, informal chat. Although it was evident from introductory training sessions that he personally conducted that he considered himself a master salesman, his style was almost the opposite of John Gable's: he enjoyed presenting himself as a worldly-wise, solid-gold success, someone who did not have to prove his toughness to anyone, but was willing to bequeath his storehouse of expertise to any worthy beneficiary.

So, after commending Paul for his laudable work habits, but pointing out the troubling fact that he nevertheless owed him at least twenty dollars, Pernell gently inquired, "Can you help me out here?"

Although Paul understood, he said, "I don't understand."

"Well, just so we get off on a good footing, so that nobody owes anyone anything, would you be willing to work for a draw of, say, three hundred dollars a week?"

"You told me the minimum guaranteed draw per week was three hundred and fifty dollars."

"I want you to be happy here, Paul. So talk to me. What can you do for me?"

"I can't work for less than three hundred and fifty dollars a week."

Paul's morale took a nosedive after that, and by the end of the second week his earnings dipped below the two hundred dollar mark. When Pernell once again invited him into his office, he was neither surprised, unprepared, nor excessively defensive. He made it a point of honor to say nothing and show as little feeling as possible when the owner informed him that although he still liked him and believed in his potential, given his precipitous decline, "I have no choice but to cut back your draw to two hundred dollars a week."

For about five weeks, while he scanned the want ads, husbanding his energy as best he could, he hung on. When he could no longer stand it, although he had no other job prospect in sight, he called up the office and announced that he was quitting, that he would be coming in only to pick up his final check.

After a long pause, the bookkeeper got on the line. "There's no check for you."

When Paul responded with bitter arguing, refusing to hang up or give in, Sid Pernell came to the phone and essentially said this: "You owe us about five hundred dollars. Not once did you make your draw. After the shit that you pulled here, you've got the nerve to ask for a check."

"I'll sue," said Paul.

"Go ahead. I've got a team of lawyers who work for me and I'll tie you up for years."

He had heard rumors that owners of boiler rooms, if they thought they could get away with it, would sometimes withhold the last paycheck of terminating employees, knowing that there were few who were willing legally to pursue their rights—but he had not thought that it could happen to him. Now that it had, his fantastic stubbornness once more kicking in,collecting the money owed him became a crusade. The following day he called the office back and left a message, directed to the attention of Sid Pernell, that he was hand-delivering a copy of the pitch he had received in his initial sales training to the office of the attorney general. Although he had no intention of doing so unless he had to, he was banking on the fact that Pernell would be understandably reluctant, if not outright fearful, at having his hokey sales gimmick laid out in cold print before the policing eyes of the people's-advocate attorney general.

Then he went directly to the office of the labor board in lower Manhattan to register an official complaint that he had been cheated out of his lawful wages for an honest week's work. It was a one-two punch that Paul hoped would spare him the trouble of legally battling Sid Pernell, but it did not work. When Mr. Robinson, the mediator who recorded the grievance, personally telephoned Pernell in an attempt to head off a complicated legal procedure if he could, he was drily instructed, "I owe him money? He owes me money!"

It did not deter Paul, who persevered in the defense of his rights. Seven weeks later, he received a letter from Robinson, advising him that after Robinson had personally visited and interviewed the owner, Mr. Pernell had consented—solely, as he insisted, to settle a nuisance claim—to pay the disputed week's wages.

Paul had won, and it was all the justification he needed to push ahead in his determination to become an outstanding and respected salesman. For the next three and a half years, he faithfully applied himself to the dictates and goals of Mitford Real Estate, a medium-sized firm that had offered, in addition to the straight-commission promises of undreamed-of riches, the pedestrian benefit of health insurance coverage pending the completion of a full year's work.

Principally through his astounding capacity for work, Paul managed consistently to tally among the top third of the room's producers, which meant only that he could almost cover his weekly expenses. He was discovering the hard way that while it is in the nature of the born salesman to claim that he is a superstar, few can consistently even make a decent living.

Unlike most salesmen, however, Paul was interested in respect, not money, and it was therefore not his low income but his low self-image that brought him to the crisis that in turn brought him to me; what he first spoke about when he first saw me was not business but romance. Specifically, his ex-girlfriend, Sarah Bogin—it was she who had put the spike through the heart of his already floundering self-esteem.

Paul diagnosed himself as being in despair. A year ago he had met someone he considered the perfect woman for him: beautiful, smart, sensitive, mysterious, she was an aspiring writer who was already publishing articles in leading women's magazines. She slept with him on the first date; told him he was her best friend on the second date; and revealed on their third date that she did not sleep with her best friends.

Once again, Paul's stubbornness kicked in. He would be her best friend if that is what she wanted him to be, until he could no longer stand it, in the hope that one day she would take him back as a lover. So he rebuilt a cabinet for her when it needed rebuilding, because that is what a best friend does, accompanied her to the ballet when she needed a companion, jogged by her side when she requested a running partner, and in spite of his considerable jealousy, forced himself to act as confidant to her intermittent romantic interludes.

But, he decided he could no longer stand it when she asked him to come with her to the drugstore—she had to purchase some sanitary napkins, and because of a lingering teenage quirk, found it easiest to do so in the company of a friend. Upon thinking it over, Paul decided such a friend he could never be, and, though comical and embarrassing in the retelling, his refusal helped clarify and define his neglected needs.

So, while earlier he had clandestinely labored to become a reinstated lover, now he boldly asserted to Sarah that nothing less would suit him: and when she responded that it was not possible for her to think of him that way again, Paul would not let himself take no for an answer.

Since it was evident that success, money, and power—based on the roster of her past and current boyfriends—was what Sarah admired, then that was what he would achieve. He was enchanted, therefore, by his acquaintance with Ralph Cavalere, unquestionably the greatest salesman he had ever encountered; and understandably disappointed when his new mentor prematurely left: but before he did, he tipped Paul on to the hottest sales shop in town, Neil's Network.

It was there, as to a second chance, that Paul turned—a huge loft area on the Upper East Side that had been divided and subdivided into geometrical rows of identical cubicles, each supplied with a telephone and a scripted sales pitch. Although this setup was by now familiar to Paul, what was different about Neil's Network, according to Ralph Cavalere, was that it provided a sound training in the fundamentals of selling, and did not just throw you into the lion's den the way most boiler rooms did.

They accomplished this by insisting on a mandatory probation period of at least six months, during which initiates would be schooled in every aspect of telemarketing a multitude of products. To remove the temptation to seek out disreputable shortcuts in order to boost sales, trainees would be placed on a straight hourly wage without commission incentive, and only after they had proven themselves over a solid six months would they be permitted to try their hand at the more lucrative straight-commission sales.

It was the kind of firm, and the kind of job, that seemed to reward patience and stamina, not greed and aggression, and to that extent it was appealing to Paul, who with a renewed sense of purpose threw himself into the task at hand, which was to read from test-marketed scripts believably and pleasantly, using Watts lines that gave him access to the homes of thousands of paid subscribers scattered across the country. The benefit of contacting only existing customers, as opposed to cold-calling only strangers, as he had been required to do at Rover Books, was immediately apparent: they were friendlier, less resistant, and therefore decidedly easier to sell, inasmuch as they had already been sold at least once before. Accordingly, there was substantially less pressure to produce sales by converting the nos of recalcitrant buyers into cash-register-ringing yeses.

But Paul was to discover, as he did at Rover Books, that there is no such thing as no pressure, and while it was true that he was now less exhausted after a five-hour shift on the telephone than he had previously been, he was still almost spent. Nevertheless, he continued to plug away in his cubicle, garnering high marks from his supervisor (as he knew he would) for his telephonic tenaciousness, but he could hardly conceal from himself that his dream of a second chance was effectively dead.

This would not be the way out, he reasoned, because how could the way out be anything so colossally boring? At least with Mitford Real Estate, although in the final analysis he had barely made a living, there was always the high-wire excitement of waiting to find out if he was going to make a sale (score) or bomb out. It may have been nerve-wracking, depressing, eventually humiliating, but it was never boring. By contrast, Paul realized that along with the advertised security of a noncommission hourly wage came the death of suspense.

If selling was supposed to be, as Ralph Cavalere had instructed him, the art of sublimated and personified conquest, what challenge could there be in persuading someone to reorder a product he was initially satisfied with? Very little, it seemed to Paul. It followed that he found it difficult (as did everyone else) to become involved in what he was enjoined to represent: an assortment of lesser-known imitations of leading brand names, such as *TV Guide*, American Express Card, *Life* Magazine, that were hoping to crash the big time via the magic of telemarketing.

The man responsible for the magic, who billed himself as the world's greatest telephone salesman, was Neil Munson, the founder of Neil's Network—a large, dour man who periodically shuffled past the rows of cubicles, occasionally stopping to chat with a toiling telemarketer, a public-relations reminder that he had not lost the human touch.

Keeping his nose to the telephone, Paul did his best to avoid such pseudo-contact, and was relieved when he was passed by. In three months' time, despite the regularity of wages, he had come to despise this job more than any he had ever had. If it were possible, he found the underhanded, understated, but pervasive manipulation he was now subjected to less tolerable than the up-front contempt of a tiny but rambunctious boiler room such as Rover Books. Whereas before he could at least fantasize about combating personal enemies, here he was up against a system that had been developed, tested, and perfected in telemarketing sites as far-flung as New York, Geneva, and Tokyo.

And the system was this: Do not waste time on such outmoded concepts as individual initiative, commission incentives, and the stimulation of competition. Do not take the risk of relying upon the unpredictable and therefore unknown factors of imagination and creativity, but instead replace them with a mass-produced, mass-tested, and therefore scientifically proven method of selling.

Which was to: establish a base rate of reorder sales per hour, a base rate of maximal output by incoming trainees before the inevitable fatigue sets in—then engineer a system that could maximize these two variables. That meant, of course, that the need for fresh recruits necessitated an operation that would force a constant turnover. New faces were always in demand (thus Neil's Network ran an ad year-round), because it had been found that short bursts of intense activity by inexperienced go-getters, who were dismissed as soon as their energy level began to drop, was far more effective than the long-term performance of experienced but tired sales personnel. But how to derive the maximum effort from employees who were guaranteed only a meager hourly wage and given no incentive whatever to excel?

The answer was plain: computerized monitoring of every single sales call, polite but unceasing pressure, and the use of standardized, pretested scripted sales pitches so as to erase the possibility of human error.

And because Paul did not know where to go, even though his dream of a second chance had expired, his morale therefore being at an all-time low, he was naturally loath to take this in. But after months had gone by, and he'd seen for himself that less than one percent of the trainees lasted more than six weeks and that no one to his knowledge had ever made the transition from probation to straight-commission salesman, it dawned on him that in four years all he had accomplished was to come full circle: to a much more sophisticated, large-scale, and impersonal version of Rover Books.

The realization that his chosen mentor, Ralph Cavalere, had therefore been toying with him by pointing him toward Neil's Network, which was nothing but a computerized Rover Books, caused his stubbornness—for the last, and perhaps most destructive, time—to kick in.

No matter what the cost, he would not accept this. When I made the suggestion (a naive one, in retrospect) that it might be simpler to get another job or try another industry, Paul brushed it aside: it was not a matter of expedience, it was a point of honor that he exact manly revenge.

After concocting and discarding many plots—secretly amassing a dossier of employee transgressions to be submitted to the attorney general's office, hiring a private detective to uncover past malfeasance, drafting an exposé for the newspapers—Paul settled on an inspired and, what I had to admit, was a diabolically clever idea.

It arose from a chance conversation with a fellow telemarketer, Marty Simon, a former professor of labor law at Brooklyn College, who enjoyed reminiscing about his heyday as a consultant and mediator for evolving labor unions. In a brilliant flash it occurred to Paul that because of its transitory part-time nature, its lack of fringe benefits, and its minimal wages, no one had ever found it advisable or worthwhile to attempt to unionize Neil's Network; and from that it followed that Neil Munson would probably be totally unprepared, and likely enraged, at anyone's attempting to do so. Sensing that Marty Simon felt as bitter toward Munson as he did, he confided his idea, which was instantly ratified. Not only that, but he could personally teach, in a couple of weekends, everything Paul would need to know properly and legally to get the ball rolling, if he were willing to be the front-line organizer, while to lend credibility, he himself would offer his name to be placed on the requisite voting ballot as first president.

Logically, of course, it made no sense to unionize a high-turnover boiler room, but as a symbolically defiant protest and Machiavellian thorn in the side of Neil Munson, "It was a hoot."

So two weeks later, after taking a crash course in unionizing protocol, Paul boldly knocked on the glass pane of Munson's office door, who, no doubt thinking it was someone else, promptly invited him in.

"Who are you?"

Paul was about to identify himself when the owner recovered.

"Oh, you work here as a telemarketer."

"Yes."

During the pause that ensued, Paul steadied himself and then plunged, with angry determination, into his prepared speech.

"I'm here, sir, at your own request. You yourself said, in the first talk I heard you give, that your door would always be open to the grievances of telemarketers."

"What is your grievance?"

"It concerns the structure of the company, and therefore applies to the rights and grievances of all telemarketers. It comes, essentially, to this: that the working conditions at Neil's Network are unfair, coercive, and abusive. The wages are minimal, there is no room for advancement, and the constant pressure from computer monitoring is inhumane. Also, false promises were made about there being an opportunity here to do lucrative straight-commission sales, which happens not to be the case, which adds up to misrepresentation."

"If you're so unhappy, why don't you quit?"

Dramatically, Paul spread a sheaf of mimeographed sheets of paper across the desk of the founder of Neil's Network.

"I've decided instead to correct these abuses by unionizing your company. Those are your copies, for your lawyer, of the labor law statutes governing the protocol for setting up a union. You know Marty Simon, the former professor of labor law at Brooklyn College, he works here. He's advising me on how to set this up."

So abashed was Munson that he could only sputter, "You're fired!"

Thrilled that he seemed for once in his life to be in control, Paul rose from his chair and authoritatively pointed first to one piece of paper, then another.

"Read the statute carefully, Mr. Munson. It's against the law to fire anyone who assumes the duties of organizing a union. If you do fire me, you'd better believe that Professor Simon and myself will prefer charges against you with the labor board, and there is no precedent of an employer's winning such a case. The other piece of paper, by the way, is a leaflet informing telemarketers of our intention to unionize Neil's Network, and urging them to vote for us when the time comes. I have a whole stack of them in my cubicle right now, and just to show you that I'm serious, at the end of my shift I'll be stationed by the door to make sure that every employee here gets one."

Without waiting for a reply, Paul stood up, nervously returned to his cubicle, and immediately resumed dialing, to calm himself down. He had been more excited in Munson's office than he could ever remember being, but whether it was from the palpitations of anxiety or the exhilarating sense of having been unbelievably brave, he didn't know. Nor did he care, as he stubbornly renewed his pledge to himself that no matter what the price, he would see this thing through to the bitter end.

And compared with that first giant step he had already taken, the rest was not so bad. What was more, now that he had officially and legally declared himself as the front-line organizer, he had Marty Simon, who was eager to help. At the end of his shift Marty, true to his promise, was standing by the entrance to the building, and together they distributed their leaflets to each of the departing telemarketers.

To a veteran of unionizing wars such as Marty Simon, what followed, while immensely and enjoyably vindictive, on the level of labor law was predictably routine. Neil Munson, as Simon knew he would, immediately handed over the stack of papers Paul had served him with to his lawyer, who advised him that he had no choice but to submit to the statutory machinery for organizing a union and let it run its course. Accordingly, a mutually agreed-upon date was specified when the employees who wished to do so could vote either for or against the creation of a union.

Until that time, as Paul was to discover in his fledgling stint as union organizer, there was much to do. In addition to the grueling five hours he normally put in on the telephone, he now was required to hand out leaflets, proselytize whenever he could to whoever would listen, and on occasion hold emergency secret meetings with Marty Simon in the hallway, or even the men's room.

Paul learned that the tension that had filled the office in his primary confrontation with Neil Munson would not die or dissipate at least until the last of the votes, on the day of decision, had been tallied. And that the labor law, which clearly favored the petitioning unionizers, nevertheless also granted employers the right to state their case directly, which is how Munson, standing on a dingy radiator facing a captive audience of bemused telemarketers, came to make the following speech:

"Many years ago, when I was an undergraduate at City College, I was in favor of unions, and the rights of employees to have a union if they wanted one.

"I still am in favor of that right. But do you want a union here? How long, how many weeks do most of you work here on the average before moving on? It's six weeks, if you want to know. That's all. And at minimum wages.

"Let's be honest. This is a part-time job. A damn good one, but a part-time job. Nobody considers this a career. Do you? You're students, or housewives, or actors, but you're not sticking around.

"So why would you want to pay dues in order to accrue bene-fits that none of you is going to be here to collect anyway?

"It makes no sense to me. Sure, there are plenty of things wrong with Neil's Network, there are valid grievances, but is a union the way to go about it—instead of a committee of your own representatives, selected by you, to meet regularly with me and my staff to air and negotiate our differences?"

Concluding, Munson jabbed at the air with his heavy forefin-ger.

"But look, if you want a union, if what I've said doesn't make sense to you, then go ahead and have your union. I didn't oppose it when I was an undergraduate at City College, and I won't oppose it now."

Both Paul and Marty Simon, who had heard a dozen such speeches in his career, concurred that it had been effective. Not for its oratory, but because it had put its finger on the fatal flaw in the proposed argument to unionize Neil's Network. It really did not make any sense to unionize a high-turnover boiler room, out-side of the malicious pleasure it afforded its instigators, and this was a point readily appreciated by their fellow telemarketers. Although nine out of ten of them vocally and belligerently despised everything about Neil's Network, almost none of them could see surrendering even a fraction of their measly salaries to the payment of union dues in order to collect benefits they would surely not be around to enjoy.

So when the moment of truth came, there was no need to rig

the voting, although Marty Simon would not have put that past Neil Munson: the majority of telemarketers declared themselves resoundingly opposed to the idea of unionizing the company.

As a final act of defiance, to get their goat, Paul continued to work as a telemarketer, to show that he could do the outrageous thing he had done, and still, protected by the labor law, be immune to firing.

Then, as he would describe it to me, on a day filled with sunshine, simply because he felt like it, he walked out of Neil's Network and never returned. Looking back upon it, it seemed as though he had never really been there, that mysteriously an enormous pressure had suddenly loosened its hold on him, and he on it.

Although he would still stubbornly solicit the romantic interest of Sarah Bogin, he would not do so in a boiler room, and he would never again aspire to be a salesman.

THE SALESMAN

In high school, a favorite teacher had taught us, as he saw it, from the idealistic vantage point of a passionate Democrat, the evolution of the American consumer's attitude toward big business. In the beginning, that attitude had been decidedly anti-business, influenced by the awareness of outrages committed by people like the first Rockefeller and the so-called original "robber barons" of the late nineteenth century. Acknowledging the problem, American industry set out in earnest to develop what was a revolutionary idea in the early twentieth century, embodied in the buzzword "public relations": intended to counteract the widespread view of American businessmen as predators upon the public, it was boosted by a second buzzword—the concept of "public service." Accordingly, as the twentieth century unfolded, American business began slowly but persistently to promote the idea that everything they do is somehow done for the benefit of the American consumer.

Since I had grown up accepting the idea (not that I especially believed it) that businessmen exist to serve the public, the revelation that such a claim might be little more than a duplicitous pose or expedient strategy was fascinating. Yet in retrospect, what is even more astonishing, in the face of nearly universal cynicism, is the degree to which this sanitized image of the American businessman is still taken for granted: at the time of this writing (1991) it shows no signs of abatement.

This is not, by the way, to imply a deprecatory view of salesmen per se; it is meant, instead, to call attention to the relationship they have been professionally enlisted to foster. If the dynamic hallmark of that relationship, as is tirelessly alleged, is really public-spirited service, then that means a definite caring and nurturing predisposition of mind must exist *prior* to the initial contact with a customer (who by definition must be a stranger). Yet simple reflection will show that true nurturance and cultivation of another's needs is a relatively advanced and delicate interpersonal transaction, and therefore almost always comes after a personal relationship has been established, hardly ever before. Unless, of course, the prototypical salesman happens to be the kind of individual who has been characterized as an especially empathic, or what is sometimes called therapeutic, personality: that is, one who has the capacity and talent to begin a relationship with a complete stranger by wisely and sensitively resonating with his needs. Yet even psychotherapists—for whom a therapeutic personality is supposedly a requisite tool of the trade—are rarely equipped, in my experience, with such a benevolent temperament.

How then can stock-in-trade salesmen, who as we know are chosen for their aggressive and proven pursuit of profitable self-advancement, ever live by such an egoless ideal as serving the public? It is a simple truth that they cannot, but it was drummed into me through working, over the past ten years, not only with aspiring business successes such as Paul, but with struggling artists, who, thinking they were merely detouring and regrouping in a temporary, stop-gap job, found themselves mired in that contemporary telemarketing sweatshop, a "boiler room."

It is my thesis that the boiler room, admittedly the underbelly and canker of large-scale corporate business, can tell us much about the respectable superstructure that smugly squats on top of it. This may be because the boiler room—analogous to the way psychosis or mental breakdown, although comparatively rare, traditionally reveals volumes about what goes on underneath the more sedate, seamless covers of the well-coordinated personality—in its unabashed, unbridled greed may dramatize what lies concealed beneath the unctuous business pretense of serving the public.

Over forty years ago an unassuming light comedy, *A Letter To Three Wives* (a film that has since become a classic), starring Kirk Douglas and Ann Southern, made its debut. In it Kirk Douglas plays a disgruntled, underpaid school teacher who conceives of himself as a passionate lover of pure literary values, and who is revolted at what he apprehends as the engulfing tidal wave of sleazy and philistine American advertising, ironically spearheaded by his wife's enterprising marketing firm. In what seemed at the time a stock melodramatic speech, Douglas lashes out at advertisers who glorify their products as not only the best, but as the solution to life's most enduring hardships.

What is remarkable after forty years is how well that speech stands up, since it in no way was meant to be prophetic, but was simply dished up as entertainment, as contemporary slick movie dialogue. And while it is true that today's advertising is often presented tongue in cheek, the message seems clear: objects are of comparable, perhaps even greater, importance than people or relationships. What advertising, marketing, and sales all promote, instead of the interpersonal relationship, is what might be called an objective relationship to the primary objects in one's immediate inanimate environment. What is attractive is the product, and what salesmen, accordingly, are primarily promoting is the *charisma of the product.* In sales, what is omnipotent is not the person but the product, and it follows that advertisements often depict human beings as being either seduced by it or under its spell.

Seen in this way, the psychology of sales is an attempt to excite the prospective buyer similarly to the way that the seducer tries to arouse the person to be seduced. Analogous to the moment of truth when the seducer (as for example in a disguised sexual seduction) frankly reveals his intent, the "close" in a well-thought-out sales pitch is carefully deferred until the buyer is believed to be optimally primed. Such behavior strongly suggests that the salesman, like the seducer, does not believe that anyone would buy his product unless he or she were sold on it first.

In this sense, selling can only be a manipulation, and the salesman can get what he wants only by hiding what he is really asking for. It follows that the salesman will relate to the buyer essentially through the product, and the buyer in turn will respond primarily through the expression of a positive or negative reaction to the proffered product-stimulus. This is a triangular relationship characterized by indirectness: one that is based solely on need and not on the person, or even the hope of intimacy. The only question, the whole point of the relationship, is whether or not an isolated need will be satisfied. The underlying assumption of sales appears to be that people are needy in a greedy way, and that when the targeted need is patiently and skillfully gratified, they are more likely than not to be seduced into buying. Since it is assumed that customers in general want as much as they can get while giving as little as possible and since salesmen have been conditioned to make as much profit as possible at the lowest possible costs, there is an uneasy awareness that the real relationship, if the ulterior motives were candidly acknowledged by both parties, will necessarily be combative and incongruent.

To dissolve the stalemate or potential escalation of such conflicting needs, the myth has been cultivated that what the salesman really wants is to service, and not sell to the customer. It is important that no matching myth has been fashioned, which would be that what the customer really wants is to service the salesman, for example, by sponsoring and endorsing his product—which, when you think of it, is no less believable than the reverse. It is hardly an accident, then, that the hypothetical consumer, by implication and omission, is encouraged to think that he will be indulged in the very best service the salesman can offer, with no obligation whatsoever to reciprocate. A picture is thereby deliberately drawn of the captivated buyer as someone who is not only free unselfconsciously to pig out on his favorite product, but who will be admired for doing so.

This portrait of the buyer, as put forward by the seller, is suggestive of the addict: but here the supposed addiction is to the product. And there is a sense, analogous to the parallel processes of seduction and addiction, in which it can be said that the sales man operates, or tries to, on a similar principle: to proceed through a series of intentionally small, nonthreatening steps to an orchestrated euphoria, with the expected toxic side effects (inability to handle payments or beneficially to utilize the product) deftly deferred. This is why salesmen talk only about product benefits, and why a sales pitch can be seen as a kind of seduction, which, when it succeeds, does so for comparable reasons. The subject is led down the garden path, tantalized by one harmless pleasure (product benefit) after another, until a mood of appetitive arousal is reached, at which point the "close" is attempted, to elicit money for something that until then had appeared almost effortlessly accessible. The salesman, like the seducer, tries to lull the buyer's understandable fear that he is the target of aggressive greed by pretending to be himself under the spell (the seducer's flattery) of an overriding wish to provide service; in other words, he is not there to take, he is there to give.

It is therefore hardly surprising that salesmen, again like seducers, will measure the potency of their persuasive powers by stacking it up against the weight of the customer's resistance. Great salesmen, like Don Juans, love to boast how they overcame seemingly impossible challenges (the diehard customer as equivalent to the virgin), and to that extent their relationships bear a nonreciprocal, predator-prey stamp. In place of communication, there is the art of misdirection and persuasion. Instead of negotiating and working things out in a spirit of mutuality, there is a determination to blot out resistance and "overcome" objections. There is also the parallel between the seduced one's retrospective sense of having shamefully participated in a corrupt, self-compromising act, and what has been called "buyer's remorse," typically occurring within forty-eight hours after the sale, when the customer figures out that he has overextended himself and not acted in his own best interest.

For all of these reasons, the underlying conception of human nature that guides the psychology of selling can be likened to a cartoon, yet one, despite the just-kidding, tongue-in-cheek disclaimers of most advertising, that deserves to be taken seriously because it says much about the sales mind, and could be fairly described as reductionism run amok. In this view, people are seen as creatures with instinctual behavioral buttons that, pressed by the appropriate motivational or subliminal stimulus, will "release" their programmed appetitive response.

Once again the question deserves to be asked: What kind of human being is it whose mood is profoundly elevated by mere proximity to a preferred product? The answer seems to be, one who is psychologically impaired, with a marked deficit of imaginative inner life, and who is therefore fixated on objects at hand. There is a remarkable similarity between this notion of human nature and that of lower animals (e.g., birds and fish) as developed by the ethologists Konrad Lorenz (1970, 1971) and Niko Tinbergen (1951): the concept of fixed action pattern, the IRM (innate releasing mechanism, a genetically programmed behavior pattern, constituted by a few key behaviors or a few principal behavioral strategies, which are triggered into play by the activation of a sign stimulus) and the releasers. In humans, from the vantage point of advertising, the IRM can be likened to an appetite for any product ever designed by a manufacturer, and the "releaser" is an image or association that effectively triggers it. Once the releaser (e.g., the shape of a car) is activated, the fixed action pattern is set in motion, so the scenario goes, and the consumer is driven to purchase and find satisfaction in the object of his desire. It is no accident that advertisements often portray the consumer as ravenous, an animal enjoying its prey, and accordingly, depict the ego of the typical customer as ludicrously weak, not to be respected, but to be dealt with through learning how to surmount objections, while the superego is relegated to the aforementioned simplistic category of "buyer's remorse."

Such a view of human nature is close to a caricature of the original psychoanalytic model of man as primarily a creature driven by id (instinct), and it carries definite implications. As such, the pitch, like the seduction, is a strategy that assumes that people are programmed according to primary needs that have to be met, and that in order to ensnare the target, it is necessary to tap into the opportune impulse. A pitch and a seduction share a deep pessimism concerning the possibility of safely, honestly, and intimately having one's needs responded to: and it follows that their intrinsic manipulation will be the antithesis of what is called symbiosis, in which surviving alone is seen as impossible. By contrast, success in sales, as in seduction (although this is routinely denied), is predicated on the impossibility of surviving together: the zero-sum belief that to the victor belong the spoils.

THE TWO
PHILOSOPHIES OF SALES

If it is true that the psychology of sales is informed by an unstated ideology and philosophy of human nature, then it is worthwhile considering it. As will be seen, the two philosophies suggested here are variations of an underlying reductionism: the attempt to reduce the complexity of human behavior to a handful of manageable rules.

The first such philosophical picture of human nature has already been alluded to as the ethological one, and it goes back at least as far as Konrad Lorenz, the father of modern ethology. It was Lorenz who most fully conceptualized the then-revolutionary idea of the fixed action pattern: that there are genetically programmed sequences of animal behaviors that once activated could continue without the slightest monitoring, feedback, or triggering of receptor-stimuli. Buoyed by his discovery, Lorenz began to speculate on a hypothesized mechanism by which the innate fixed action pattern might get triggered and then implemented.

He would eventually arrive, together with Nicholas Tinbergen, at his concept of the innate releasing mechanism (IRM). This would be something like a genetically keyed response to a skeletally simple, primal stimulus in the animals' average expectable environment. Lorenz offers the analogy of a key fitting into a lock. The releasing stimulus must be relatively simple, and it must be representative of basic environmental experience so as to carry selective, adaptive survival value: and according to Lorenz, this is what a key fitting into a lock does.

Yet, as wonderful and simple as all this appears, Lorenz warns that the naive observer tends to overestimate the amount of information contained in the IRM genetic program. To make this point, he cites the example of a newly hatched turkey, which instantly crouches and goes under cover at first sight of a hawk flying over; or of a young kestrel, which, on first encountering water, bathes and preens itself as expertly as if it had done these things hundreds of times. Lorenz duly notes that such examples are impressive, then wryly adds, "To see turkey chicks react in the same manner to a fat fly slowly crawling along the ceiling, or the young kestrel trying to bathe, using the same movements, on a polished marble table, is actually disappointing" (1981, p. 158). Yet he concludes that such errors eventually helped to lead to a better understanding of the parsimony of the information contained in the IRM.

Inspired by Lorenz, Tinbergen, in a series of ingenious experiments, demonstrated the surprising simplicity of key stimuli (releasers) and at the same time their additive effect. Of all the releasers subsequently studied by ethologists, perhaps none became as famous as the one involved in the process discovered by Lorenz: the mysterious IRM by which young members of certain species, during highly sensitive, critical ontogenetic phases of development, suddenly and "irreversibly"—upon the arrival of certain key stimuli—imprint the various responses appropriate to their own biological mother. The fact that the IRM involved in imprinting could spectacularly backfire—that a man, by bending low and issuing a certain rhythmic cackle, could so successfully imitate the key stimuli that he would become "imprinted" as the mother—made the process all the more wonderful. If there is an abiding image of Konrad Lorenz, it is of him being followed by greylag goslings who have "imprinted" him as their mother.

Although he was profoundly devoted to the animal world, Konrad Lorenz was aware of the appropriation by advertisers of his concepts of the IRM and the releaser, and was prescient enough to write:

Most measures taken by fashion to enhance female—and male—beauty function on the principle of exaggerated key stimuli. The same is true of the doll industry. Humans respond with emotions and behavior patterns of parental care to a number of configurational key stimuli that can easily be analyzed—and also exaggerated. One of them is a high and slightly bulging forehead, a brain case large in proportion to the face (as in a baby) and visceral cranium, large eyes, rounded cheeks, short and stubby limbs and a rounded fat body. Additional key stimuli are uncertain, stumbling movements (1981, p. 164).

In the high-speed world of print and TV media—where the product is exposed only for seconds—it is understandable that auditory and visual subliminal cues considered to be powerful behavioral "releasers" will be employed.

If such an ethological picture of human responsiveness represents one kind of philosophical reductionism informing the strategy of selling, then the "theory of games" represents another.

Historically, the theory of games arose out of a conceptual union between two disparate disciplines when John von Neumann, the mathematician, and Oskar Morgenstern, the economist, collaborated to produce a seminal work, *The Theory of Games and Economic Behavior* (1944). The idea was to extend mathematics into a new realm, while simultaneously securing for economics a solid mathematical foundation. In order to do this, they proceeded to shrink the rich diversity of economic interplay down to what they called a zero-sum game, i.e., somebody wins and somebody loses, and further proceeded to reduce the multitude of real-life economic participants down to just a couple of hypothetical game players.

With this toy model of the world of economics in hand, von Neumann began to explore the various mathematical combinations of winning moves or strategies by which one economic player might alternatively team up (or not) with a second player in order to extract gain from a third player. Deceptively, with this minimal cast and with an elegance characteristic of his genius,

John von Neumann, together with Morgenstern, created a series of winning economic strategies, which—at the fundamental mathematical level on which they were postulated—worked beautifully.

These ideas caught on and were extended to fields other than mathematics and economics. The way game theory analyzed human behavior into an adversarial system of serialized, discrete components or "moves," and then proceeded to devise winning (adaptive, cooperative) strategies, had a wide appeal.

Game theory was brought into the biological sciences by the evolutionary biologist, John Maynard Smith (1972), when he introduced his now famous concept of an evolutionary stable strategy (ESS). It was no accident that Smith was both a mathematician and a biologist, since his idea of an ESS was a revolutionary wedding of the mathematical theory of games and the growing biological field of population genetics. An evolutionary stable strategy is one that, once it has gained ascendancy in a given population of a given species, cannot be ousted by any competing or mutant strategy. An ESS is not necessarily conscious: just how unconscious an ESS can be is best illustrated by the fact that W. B. Hamilton, another leading evolutionary biologist, has taken the idea of an ESS all the way down to the level of bacteria (1981). An ESS can be thought of as a simple, formal series of behaviors conferring an adaptive biological advantage over evolutionary time that has been programmed by natural selection into the genome.

Eric Berne, who was chiefly responsible for introducing game theory into ego-psychology with his hugely popular *Games People Play* (1964), shrewdly named his interpersonal ego-psychology interactions "transactions," thereby opening the way to a more rigorous, game-like way of looking at behavior.

There is a profound difference between the game theorist and the psychoanalytic approach to studying patterns of human behavior. To the psychoanalyst, conflict, as well as being external and cognitive, can be internal, intrapsychic, intersystemic, and this is almost never the case with game theorists (except, appropriately, Berne). Game theorists, by contrast, almost always picture conflict externally, between adversaries, or, if internally, as a battle between competing tempting cognitive choices. This is another way of saying that conflict to the game theorist is a rational dilemma.

Again by contrast, the patterns of human behavior teased apart by psychoanalytic investigation, although sometimes beautiful and precise, have nothing mathematical, logical, or even necessarily cognitive about them. Instead, they are shot through with meaning, intrapsychic as well as interpersonal, and have little if anything to do with the hypothesized costs and benefits or cognitive, adaptive strategies of game theorists.

As Berne (1964) showed, there is scarcely anything intimate about game-like human behavior. Game theorists have little to say about emotions, and generally do not allow for motivation other than the presumed flat, logical one of rationally opting for the most advantageous cost-benefit ratio strategy. While it is true that game theory considers bad strategies, bad games, bad gamesmanship, it does not seem to allow for the deeper, more self-defeating and stubbornly irrational behavior that has been described in psychoanalysis as "repetition compulsion." The psychoanalyst, unlike the game theorist, when studying game-like human behavior by no means makes the assumption that the player is playing to win the game.

Seen in this light, from the psychoanalytic standpoint it is the intrusion of irrationality that is sorely missing from the depiction of behavior by game theorists. Once a behavioral game starts, it doesn't self-interrupt, unless such an interruption is itself a programmed game move. In games there is no such thing as a Freudian slip; the game once started generally runs through to completion. Games seem to presuppose an intact person as player: we do not hear of schizoid games, ambivalent games, guilt-ridden games. Once the game has begun, conflict seems to be mainly external, between opposing strategies and opposing players. Internal conflict seems to be a matter of cognitive choice and problem-solving, of finding the optimal strategy. Therefore, in game theory, while conflict may be internal, it does not seem to be intrapsychic in the psychoanalytic sense of one psychic state being in opposition to another. In such a smoothed-out world as that of the game theorist, there does not seem to be room for free association or spontaneity of behavior.

All of which sounds suspiciously familiar, and it should come as no surprise that the majority of salesmen that I have encountered are game players and (unconscious) amateur game theorists. I do not mean merely that they tend to relate to others manipulatively and strategically, but that underlying such behavior is a genuine reductionist belief that what people do can be broken down into an explanatory battery of key motivations that, if opportunistically directed, can result in a personal payoff.

Accordingly, salesmen often approach the field of human relations like embattled logicians, armed with sales pitches that are little more than strategic snares: there is a bait (selling gambit, opening line, offer of a freebie, recitation of product benefits), a decoy, and a springing of the trap (the close). And seen this way, as a combative, zero-sum strategy (somebody wins, somebody loses), it is understandable that success in sales is frequently experienced as, and equated with, a "score" or conquest.

What the boiler-room phenomenon reveals is sales with the gloves off. Because there are no fringe benefits and few protected rights of employees, employers are relatively free to act out their aggressive impulses and fantasies in the boldest and greediest manner. The boiler-room entrepreneur, therefore, can dispense with the polite practice in blue-chip industries of enticing prospective employees with promises of future career benefits, and offer instead not security but the pleasure of participating in the hunt and (if they are true superstars) in the joy of the kill. Contempt for the consumer is widespread in boiler rooms, and because of it, idealistic salesmen such as Paul, who need to believe in their product so as to feel good about the service they deliver, are ridiculed.

Although such a concept of selling is frankly hedonistic, and is a case in point of what I call narcissistic honesty, there is a sense in which it is more honest than the corporate business persona, which professes to have committed itself to the selfless, nonaggressive goal of servicing the needy and deserving customer. While aggression is acknowledged in corporate advertising, it is acknowledged solely in the sense of aggressively competing with competitors (often portrayed as frustrated and cutthroat) in order better to serve the all-good, expectant customer. Uninhibited aggression in businessmen is thereby identified, perhaps in order to lend a compensating sense of reality to unreal-sounding sales pitches and advertising campaigns, but it is displaced and projected from its true source—between salesman and customer—to one remove away, between competitor and competitor. And it is sanitized as being no more dangerous than aggression in the service of serving the customer—or, in the language of seduction, two suitors competing for one woman's hand.

Many of the covert elements of selling, therefore, surface with disconcerting clarity in the boiler room. Here there is no pretence, as there is in established corporations, of treating the needs of the employee seriously, and here there is no union, not even the possibility of forming a union. In this sense, as in the case of Neil's Network, unions may be looked upon as a retaliatory attempt collectively and legally to coerce mutuality. It follows that in the miniature and of necessity non-unionized boiler room, where there are no effective sanctions against the expression of unalloyed aggression, the true nature of the employer is allowed to emerge. By contrast, large companies, even ones without unions, must be wary of public opinion, and therefore make a concerted public relations attempt at least to pacify new employees with talk of long-term career benefits (narcissistic giving).

It is noteworthy that other than such talk, which typically does not survive the orientation period, there is no further mention of serving the contracted employee. For the roles have now reversed, and the employer, who wants the salesman to sell to the consumer, in terms of the actual hiring and contracting of labor has become a buyer. And it is illuminating to see how the company, completely dropping its hypocritical praise of the customer as all good and always right, once it has been put in the position of the buyer, immediately becomes freely and aggressively demanding. Ironically, although the company is permitted to switch from seller (to the public) to buyer (from its employees), the hired salesman is constrained to play only one role.

But there is a twist. While the salesman is always to be a salesman, he is given a double message: on the one hand, he is to pretend to be serving the needs of the public while taking as much from it as he can; on the other hand, in his capacity as employee, he is supposed to be highly motivated to serve the employer by doing the best job he can. Although such service is allegedly rewarded in the long run, it seems clear that the salesman is meant essentially to fulfill the employer's, not the employee's needs: and consequently, it is only when the employer has been fully convinced that his needs have been met (i.e., that he has gotten much more than he has given), does he deign to offer even a partial reward.

This is one of the covert elements in sales that surfaces in the boiler room: where it is recognized that it is impossible for the salesman to be avaricious to the customer, as he is encouraged to be, yet be selfless toward the employer. Hence boiler-room entrepreneurs such as John Gable, although they traditionally love to wave the carrot ("You like money, kid?"), make no bones about the necessity of using every means to manipulate, and *force*, if they can get away with it, the fresh-faced sales recruit to work to the point of exhaustion.

While admittedly this is a long way from the ingratiating public-relations persona of blue-chip corporations, it may still be true that the best way to understand what makes a given company, large or small, tick is not to listen to their sales pitch or their advertising campaign, but to work for them. Inasmuch as company and customer, at different times, are both buyers, they are linked; and inasmuch as each views the other suspiciously as being primarily self-serving, they have both colluded, in order to avoid unpleasant confrontation, in relating as indirectly as possible to one another. Part of that may be attributed to the widespread perception that it is much harder to give as a buyer (per-haps because buyers have the money, and therefore the power) than as a seller, who accept that you have to work for what you get—which is why it is rare in American advertising for con-sumers to be portrayed as meeting anyone's needs but their own.

But there is no collusion, because there is no reason to be indi-rect where power flows only one way, in a boiler room; and accordingly, one thing that emerges with chilling clarity from the standpoint of the salesman is the degree to which pressure and selling go hand in hand. This is a natural consequence of three factors: there is no need, because of the absence of sanctions, to inhibit the demands made upon employees; there is no interest in the needs of the individual salesman; and there is sufficient concentration of power in the hands of a few to make such a pro-gram (however punitive) work. In the wildly escalated manic pressure-cooker atmosphere of the boiler room there is equal contempt for the prospective customer ("the mark") and the dis-pensable, revolving-door trainee. But there is also another kind of contempt, although greatly refined, which is deliberately muted and hidden under the "service" concept of mainstream American selling.

While it is therefore surely no accident that it has been called "high-pressure sales," this term obscures the fact there is no such thing as nonpressure sales. There is high and there is low, but there is always pressure. It exists because in selling, as in seduc-ing, it is necessary to psych oneself up to perform: to counteract the nagging sense that the relationship one is endeavoring to palm off (of primarily servicing the customer's needs) is so frag-ile, unreal, and artificial that only an overwhelming display of animation can possibly bring it off. Seen in this light, the often astonishing energy of the high-pressure salesman is mobilized not merely to overcome and swat down customer objections, but to breathe life and believability into what is essentially a cartoon professional role. One way this is done is via the osmosis of mania. If someone is as excited as the person on the other end of the telephone seems to be, then perhaps, instead of being just

THE BOILER ROOM

another gimmick, it is genuine: i.e., the target is responding to something human, alive, and authentically appealing. And in the unconscious of the customer may appear this equation: the excessive responsiveness, because it is so strong, can be caused only by a real stimulus, and not by a fake or premeditated one.

In sum, sales can be divided into high and low pressure. The high-pressure salesman, in his more transparent contempt for the buyer, can be likened to the sexual Don Juan who is interested only in the quick score, the one-night stand, while the low-pressure salesman, in his yearning for the repeat customer, is like the more temperate seductive personality who wishes to establish a tolerably corrupt but still ongoing relationship. And finally, the fanatical refusal of the high-pressure salesman, such as Ralph Cavalere, to take no for an answer can be compared, in another, more theatrical, context, with the grandiose aggressiveness of the charismatic personality such as Tony Thunder.

WHY SELLING SELLS

What is amazing is not that these crude techniques work, but that they work as well as they do. It is suggested that they work because:

- The practice of relating in a seductive, manipulative, and pressuring way is a mainstay of dysfunctional families, as well as of educational systems, and is therefore familiar.
- It is rare in any setting (familial, educational, or interpersonal) to achieve intimacy that is not tainted with recognizable seductiveness.
- It is easier in many ways to be led along and manipulated than to be autonomous and initiate a worthwhile relationship.
- In order to say no to a tempting, but patently provocative, overture, it is first necessary, but more difficult, to face oneself.
- The undoubted effort it takes to pressure and persuade someone of anything is a form of paying attention to him, which in a perverse manner can be gratifying.
- People are lonely. If someone really seems badly to want something from them, it can make them feel important and needed.
- By angrily dealing with feelings of being manipulated, one does not have to deal with feelings of intimacy. A pseudo-relationship, based on defense and retaliation, which is relatively safe can be carried on indefinitely.
- It affords one the opportunity to engage in counter-games

(Berne) with people, and to escape further from the prospect of intimacy.

- By becoming involved, whether in collusion or with a sense of protest, in the fast lane of high-pressure sales, anxiety concerning inner deprivation and an absence of intimacy can be readily projected. And an underlying confusion and dread about how to relate can thereby be converted into an absorbing narcissistic battle about how one wants to be, and wants not to be, related to.

In summary, sales, with its battery of pressuring, seductive, and exploitative strategies, can often become distorted into a relationship that at bottom is founded on aggressive, intrusive greed: to get as much from the other person as one possibly can, while giving as little as possible. When that is the case, the sales relationship is the polar opposite of intimacy, with its primary emphasis on nurturing mutuality. Yet, because it so deeply reflects the deficiency of intimacy that is so characteristic of so many types of contemporary relationships—despite its farcical, patent, and offensive artificiality—it rings strangely true, and although routinely resisted, it is so widely tolerated as to be nearly ubiquitous in our society.

PART III

LONELY HEARTS
OF MANHATTAN

THE SINGLES SCENE

It was peculiar. Emily could not remember anything that peculiar happening to her before. She had set the radio alarm for midnight, which would be plenty of time for even Charlie to arrive home from one of his interminable sales meetings and telephone her as he used to; but he had not, and she did not need the ringing of the alarm to remind her that once more he had let her down. For about a month she had called steadily, leaving numerous messages on his answering machine,with no reply. In spite of the wall of silence he had erected between them, she was certain that he still loved her, but, like every good man she had ever met, he was frightened of his own feelings, and probably terrified of intimacy.

And Charlie was a good man. He was stocky—no, fat—balding, with the kind of gruff, extroverted humor she had thought she could never find appealing. Yet somehow, despite the gulf separating their personalities, something had clicked, and shortly before her fortieth birthday she had accepted him as only the second lover she had ever had, yielding to his constant pressure (after four months of platonic dating) to engage in what she still shyly, euphemistically referred to as "the ultimate thrill." Although disappointed with his reaction, she was hardly surprised when Charlie, while acting disarmed by her sudden sexual openness, proceeded to retreat, becoming affectionate in a fatherly way rather than amorous, protective rather than aggressive, and seemingly more involved than ever in his multiple (and to her enigmatic) business ventures. Emily had been through such turnabouts before, and she reacted as she usually did, countering each new withdrawal with an empathic but insistent logic, which doggedly sought to illuminate the unacknowledged fear.

To no avail. For several weeks after their initial lovemaking Charlie had tried to reason with Emily, explaining that he was not a man to be taken so seriously, that while sleeping with her meant more than just sex, it did not mean the same thing to him as it did to her, and though he genuinely cared for her, he was in no position to offer the long-term stable relationship she evidently craved. And then, claiming that he was frustrated at being unable to communicate his point of view and needed a break, he abruptly stopped returning her telephone calls altogether.

What was peculiar, therefore, was not that he had once again failed to respond to her message—not even when she had allowed herself to say for the first time that she really *needed* to speak with him—but what had happened to the clock radio. For several hours after the alarm had sounded, she had reawakened in what must have been the dead of night and been startled, as she automatically glanced at the clock, to observe that the hands were still poised at midnight. Since the clock was in running order, that was peculiar. Almost as though someone, or some force, had moved the hands back as a signal that though Charlie had not called, time had not yet run out. It was reassuring, in a spooky way, and although she did not believe it, it enabled her finally to fall soundly asleep.

At about nine-thirty in the morning, to the chirping of birds in the courtyard behind the bedroom window of her ground-floor apartment, Emily awoke in a panic and, as if she knew, stared at the eerie hands of the psychic clock. Twelve o'clock. To verify that she was not losing her mind she dialed the number that announced the correct time (nine thirty), and then sat on the edge of her bed watching five minutes of recorded time accurately tick by, proving that the clock was working. So the hands had moved forward and then backward, and what else could it mean but that there was still time for her and Charlie? She hurried to deliver the good news, leaving six messages, one right after the other, on Charlie's answering machine, and then waited in bed for about two hours.

She could hardly think: her thoughts seemed to be jumping around like the hands of her clock, and she began to wonder if *that* were a message too. Then the hands said twelve—noon, not midnight—and she was sure she was being told it was her time now, time to act. She picked up the telephone and called Bruce, a mechanical draftsman in a graphic arts shop, who in recent months had lent a friendly confidant's ear to her tales of romantic distress.

"Something peculiar is happening to me."

"What is it, Emily?" Hie sounded concerned.

"Well, I set my radio alarm for midnight in case I fell asleep. I was hoping Charlie would return my call. The alarm went off. I got up, saw that he hadn't called, and went back to sleep. Around three in the morning, I woke up and looked at the clock. It said midnight! I checked to see if it was running. It was. I went back to sleep and woke up again at nine thirty. Guess what, Bruce? The hands said midnight."

"I don't get it."

"Those hands are jumping back and forth. I don't know who's doing it, maybe Charlie, but something's going on."

When the pause on the other end continued uncomfortably, Emily inquired, "Can we meet tonight and talk?"

"Sure."

Over coffee in a Third Avenue diner, to her increasingly puzzled friend, Emily tried to make sense of her thoughts, which persisted in jumping.

"I really think, Bruce, that Charlie came into my room while I was sleeping and kept turning those hands back to midnight. What other explanation is there?

"When I was walking over here tonight a man stopped in the middle of the street, right in front of me, and conspicuously pulled out a pack of Camels and lit one. Then, a few blocks later, I saw a cat run out from under a car. Almost right after that I thought I heard thunder, looked up, and saw some dark clouds.

And then a man with a crewcut, the kind they used to wear in the fifties, deliberately brushed my arm.

"Now don't tell me that's a coincidence. Camels ... cat ... clouds ... crewcut ... Charlie all begin with a C. It must mean something."

If it did, it was beyond Bruce's power of comprehension. Fearing for Emily's sanity, he waited for the moment when he could least awkwardly excuse himself.

There was no one to turn to now but her father in the Bronx, who, responding to her SOS, traveled to her apartment the following morning. He listened carefully to everything she said, as he always did, but try as he might he could not understand the cause and the meaning of her state of alarm.

What Emily remembered next was her father disappearing to make a series of furtive telephone calls to relatives and friends of the family, one of whom was an internist. It was this man, she believed, who met her at Lenox Hill Hospital, along with her father, who had insisted that she go.

She did not think she was hallucinating, although the psychiatrist who had interviewed her, after conferring with her father, had used that word. She was confused, yes, very confused in her thinking, but she did not think she was schizophrenic—although the psychiatrist had used that word too—and also she knew that she was not paranoid. It was true that she was suspicious to the point of embarrassment when it came to the possibility of next-door neighbors eavesdropping, and took excessive precautions, such as periodically shushing her visitors, especially if they were men, so as to shield her privacy from prying ears. That was not paranoid, that was making sure that no one who did not have a right to could know her business. And no one could tell her that she had imagined or hallucinated the hands of the clock stopping, going forward, and then returning to twelve o'clock. Charlie, someone, something had pushed those hands back, and she would never believe that she herself had unconsciously done it, as she suspected the psychiatrist was implying. But while she certainly did not trust the doctors and nurses at Lenox Hill

Hospital, she trusted her father, and felt too depleted anyway to oppose signing the admission papers that were put in her hands.

It was here, at the darkest moment in her life, when she was led to a closed ward to be joined by her putative brothers and sisters in madness, that her insistent logic, that force of mind she prided herself on, rallied to save her. She would not let the two weeks she spent there poison the hopes she had raised for herself: somehow she would banish the somnolent masklike faces, babbling voices, and wandering hands that made her flesh crawl in memory, and even in dreams. Although it did little more than sedate and settle her thoughts, she would continue to take the Haldol in minimal dosages, as prescribed by the psychiatrist.

What mattered was the vow she had made and the goal she had set. It was not unreasonable to want, even to expect, marriage by her forty-first birthday, especially for someone who had never been married. Or at least to have met, and to know that she had met, the right man, by that relatively late point in her life. Not only for her father, who had been worried for many years that his daughter would never get married, but for herself, because she had always equated true love with commitment, and in her idealistic veiw, there was only one kind of commitment that counted.

Except that until now she had been too frightened to pursue what she really needed—and now she had seen what could happen from hanging on to the wrong man.

I first met Emily about six months after she had been released from Lenox Hill Hospital, when she was well into her obsession to find the perfect love; nothing less could satisfy her standards, and perhaps relieve her underlying insecurity that only an exemplary man could find her acceptable. For while she did not look anything like the haunting burned-out chronic schizophrenics she had seen and described shuffling around the ward, she imparted the unmistakably forlorn air of someone who had weathered, but been prematurely aged by an almost unbearable psychological stress. To show the difference between what she once was, and was still in spirit if not in appearance, she brought in a framed photograph, taken when she was twenty-eight, and had just won the first of what would be several awards for creative excellence in graphic arts design. What was most striking, what made it seem like a face in a film by Ingemar Bergman, was not the unquestionably beautiful woman she had been, but the way shadow and light vied for her countenance. Even then it was impossible to tell whether she was emerging from darkness or returning to it, and to me, that was a prescient photographic metaphor of a psychological ambivalence that was to trouble her increasingly as she grew older.

The ambivalence was evident in her conflicting account of the reasons that had brought her to therapy. On the one hand, she did not believe, and had never believed, in a personal need for psychotherapy, and prided herself on a singular ability to make and carry out the difficult decisions she considered necessary. Nor did she look forward to the prying and probing which she understood the process of therapy invariably entailed. On the other hand, she had been pressured by a friend, Bruce, and advised by the psychiatrist who monitored her prescription for Haldol, that seeing a therapist could be useful as a preventive measure.

Her immediate reason for coming had been a particularly humiliating experience in a situation where she least expected it. On what seemed a typical Saturday evening, she had gone to the Revelers, a singles meeting place she had been attending regularly, and had been startled when Calvin McGraph, the proprietor, with whom she had been at least nominally friendly, had accosted her. "You know, maybe you should go home, Emily. You look awful."

And too crushed to defend herself in the forthright manner she customarily displayed against unfair attacks, Emily did go home, where she dashed into the bathroom to reexamine and reconsider the face that she had always thought looked best without makeup. Maybe the furrows in her forehead and the creases that extended from the base of her nose and curved around the corners of her mouth would look less noticeable with cosmetics, and maybe the strained look in the eyes (not yet of course the hollow stare of the burned-out schizophrenics who had tried to befriend her) would look brighter with artificial highlighting.

Although panic that she might be physically deteriorating was what impelled her to see me, a deep-seated confusion as to the strategy or process by which one procures an ideal partner was an even more compelling motivation to enter therapy.

Yet it was not something Emily wanted to face, certainly not collaboratively, and from the beginning I realized that my role was to be as a stand-by, support system against the dread of rehospitalization, and facilitater to the obsession she was determined to live out. It was not unlike the position I was in when Paul came to see me, shortly before he resolved to accomplish the impossible and unionize Neil's Network. And while therapists cannot choose the roles that are thrust upon them, nor the turning points at which they arrive in the narrative of the patient's life, I would have preferred the vantage point I enjoyed with Matthew: a survivor of a psychological holocaust, in comparatively good shape, who was eager to start anew.

Such was not the case with Emily, who felt that her second chance had passed long ago, and what remained, if anything, was a last chance. So it was more necessary than ever before, because more was at stake, to do things in her own exacting way, and that entailed relegating me to the supporting cast, along with Bruce, her father, and the psychiatrist.

Although not my choice, it was a position I was familiar with, and I did what I could. On my side was the fact that Emily genuinely liked me, trusted me as much as she was capable of, and in addition was apparently responding quite favorably to her minimal dosages of Haldol: I was relieved to see no vestiges of the outbreak of thought disorder that had landed her in the Lenox Hill Hospital psychiatric ward. That is, no vestige except one. For despite our innumerable discussions, reworkings, and recreation of her *peculiar* night, nothing could remove her fixed idea that something telepathic, extrasensory, or telekinetic had moved those clock hands. She would concede, finally, that neither

Charlie nor anyone else had come into her room, that the Camels, the cat, the clouds and crewcut, and the myriad of other unnerving conjunctions had been natural and nonmalevolent coincidences, but she could not accept that there had been no magical or spooky interference with the hands of her radio alarm.

Even if I could not shake her fixed paranoid idea, if that's what it was, it did not worry me nearly as much as the spectacle of her obsession to find the perfect love not only playing itself out before my eyes, but gradually climbing to a crescendo. For, true to the vow she had made to herself in the dark hours of her confinement, Emily was fanatically determined to do everything she could, to expend her last drop of energy, if necessary, in pursuit of the perfect mate.

And when I asked her, being genuinely curious, what qualities went into the making of such a candidate, it was as though she were waiting to give an answer she had known for a long time. A perfect lover, for her, would be, first of all, well, "a very nice guy." That was important, because while it didn't sound like much, the plain fact was that most men were not nice. They had sex on the brain, for one thing. They were not interested in feelings, and therefore not interested in communicating. There was too much "bullshit" around. That was something she was learning from attending singles functions. No one ever said what he meant. The right man, therefore, would be a composite of these things. Someone who could look past the fact that she was forty, past the face that had lost much of its beauty, and into the very special depth of feelings that was her gift, and the deep love waiting to be liberated.

Where to find such a man was the question to which she had yet to find an answer, and not for lack of trying. Immediately following her release from Lenox Hill Hospital, Emily had literally forced herself, in spite of her extreme shyness and against the advice of her psychiatrist, to participate in the singles scene. Approaching this task as she did all others—organizationally—she had proceeded to collect and study the social events listed in the classified back pages of *The Village Voice,* exclusive advertisement compilations such as *The Metropolitan News,* and direct-mail newsletters such as *The Tri-State Singles.*

Although it ran counter to her instincts, Emily decided, in order to compensate for her embarrassing lack of experience, to experiment with them all. Not surprisingly, the initial encounters were some of the most memorable, which, with her typically excellent recall, she described this way:

"I wanted to feel safe, because I felt so terribly anxious at the prospect of my first outing, so I picked a cultural event. It was a talk given at the Postgraduate Center for Mental Health on issues that were supposed to come up regularly in dating situations, and it was delivered by a resident psychoanalyst, a very nice middle-aged woman who seemed eager to make contact with the community at large. She made a point of speaking in very simple, non-technical language. I suppose the idea was to combine something cultural with something social, to interest as many people as possible so as to spread the name of the Postgraduate Center for Mental Health.

"For my part, I had come for two reasons. First, I did want to hear what this woman had to say. Maybe she could help me understand, or figure out, why I've made my mistakes with men. But the most important reason was to meet a man. Perhaps, I thought, someone who would be interested enough to attend a lecture by a psychoanalyst would be the kind of serious, patient person willing to take the time necessary to get to know me.

"It was my debut on the 'singles scene,' and my first disappointment, my first big eye-opener. I had no idea the atmosphere could be so depressing. Besides myself, only six people came to the lecture, most of whom looked between fifty and sixty years old. There were two men; one kept eating fruit he had wrapped in aluminum foil and carried in a brown paper bag, and the other, who fell asleep shortly after the psychoanalyst began to speak.

"Even though afterward I had felt like I had been with a collection of social shut-ins enjoying a communal night out, I continued to attend the Postgraduate Center lecture series. Maybe I hung on well past the time I realized I was not about to meet any interesting, available men there because I was afraid to try something new. What gave me the incentive to move on was an absolutely amazing talk called 'Lover Shopping at Bloomingdale's.'

"I don't remember the man's name, but he had been written up in *Newsweek* and *Time* magazine, and believe it or not, he was sincere. He and about twenty of his clients would actually meet in the morning outside of Bloomingdale's, divide up into teams, and disperse into different areas of the store. They would then practice the various techniques and strategies that he had taught them as to how to meet and pick up a lover anywhere, even in a big-city department store. At the end of the day they would regroup and discuss the day's failures and successes.

"Maybe because such a thing was so alien and repulsive to me, I found it fascinating in a perverse sort of way. How could this man, who was thirtyish and in no way impressive looking as far as I was concerned, think that he could overcome any barrier any woman might raise? Yet that is what he did think. To demonstrate it, he invited a volunteer, a woman who expressed frustration over her inability to handle the slightest rejection, to come onstage, and in a reversal of roles, to do her best to discourage him.

"It did not impress me that he had an immediate comeback for every rejection this woman could think up, because I thought the answers were awfully superficial. I know I'm shy, but if I don't have anything serious to say, I'd rather not say anything.

"After 'Lover Shopping at Bloomingdale's' I stopped attending lectures. I enjoyed laughing at what I had seen, but I had to admit that my own strategies and schemes for meeting someone were not getting me anywhere either. In two months I had not had a single date. I wouldn't give my telephone number out to anyone who looked in the least bit untrustworthy, and the few men I did give it to for some reason did not call. Also, I had a habit of almost immediately telling men who approached me that I was interested in starting a new relationship only as friends—until I got to know them much better—and that always seemed to dampen their enthusiasm.

"So I decided to try another place that I had heard about, the Unitarian Church. You always hear about somewhere to go that's supposed to be better than where you are. The Unitarian Church, on the Upper East Side, was supposedly an updated version of the Universalist Church, which had been one of the most popular singles get-together scenes in the mid-seventies.

"The first time I went, I took Bruce along, as a chaperon. It was a completely secular affair, located in the basement of the church. The area was huge. There must have been about two hundred people milling around when I arrived. You were supposed to sign up for the workshop or discussion group of your choice, go to it, and then socialize afterward. The idea was that you would first get a chance to meet people naturally, and then could follow up socially afterward.

"It sounded like a good idea to me. They had every conceivable workshop and discussion group—gestalt, confrontational, consciousness-raising, dance therapy, encounter experiences, you name it. I chose 'Who calls—who pays?' I hoped it would provide answers to questions I had already thought about, and it seemed a safe enough topic.

"Once again I was terribly disappointed. About twelve of us sat in a circle in straight-backed wooden or aluminum chairs and one by one, in a go-around, voiced our opinions. Some people talked a blue streak, but I said next to nothing, and everything I heard I could describe in one word—'bullshit.'

"I didn't feel like socializing afterward and I looked for Bruce, but he seemed to be having a great time talking to some women. So I kept circling around the fringe of the crowd, so as to avoid anyone approaching me. If I saw a man from my group trying to catch my eye, I pretended I didn't see him, and started nonchalantly walking in another direction. There's an expression people use about the singles scene that you've probably heard: 'the meat market.' It's true. People really do stand around and inspect each other as if they were slabs of meat. And when they talk to one another, it doesn't sound like a normal conversation, it sounds like they're buying or selling a product. It's disgusting.

"But as long as I could get Bruce to go with me, I went back, and besides, I had no place else to go. I told myself I was only looking for one man, and if ninety-nine were wrong for me but one was right, I had succeeded.

"To improve my chances, I entered workshops I customarily would not be interested in. One was called 'Personal Space. His and Hers.' I thought it was a talk group, but it turned out to be an encounter experience, where perfect strangers practiced touching one another's bodies. That's something I can't stand. The leader was a tall, striking-looking man with a flowing white blouse, like a gypsy, and he was rumored to be a well-known radical therapist. He wasted no time in enticing a volunteer, an attractive young woman with long blond braids, to lie down on her back in the middle of the room. Then he began exploring her stomach muscles with his fingers in order to locate the source of her postural tension. He did the same thing with her neck, her jaw bones, and her shoulders. Then, cupping his palms under her jaws while she was still flat on her back, he started pulling on her head. I was surprised at how unafraid and cooperative the woman was. I was waiting for her to resist, but she didn't move a muscle. After a minute of this, he released her head and announced, 'She's two inches taller now.'

"As long as it was someone else being touched or stretched, I didn't mind, but I knew that was going to change. When the leader told us to find a partner, pair off, and lie down, I felt panicky. When he said he was going to turn off the lights and that he wanted us to explore the body of our partner in ways that felt mutually comfortable, I knew I had to get out of there fast. So as soon as the light went out, I quickly stood up and tried to tiptoe out of the room without making it obvious what I was doing, but of course I made some noise, and I heard laughter behind me.

"Everyone says if you keep going to the same singles place, sooner or later you're bound to have a bad experience, and you had better be prepared for it. So far I had been disappointed, depressed, shocked a little bit, but I hadn't been seriously upset yet. My turn came after about the sixth straight visit, when I attended a group discussion called 'The Me that I Project—The Me that I Really Am.'

"I had made sure, because of my experience with the personal-space encounter, that only conversation would be involved, and it seemed tame enough. There were fourteen people in the group, and right from the start I was attracted to a slightly built, boyish-looking man who sat across from me. Randolph was his name. He seemed intense in the introverted way that I like, and I couldn't wait for him to open up.

"When his turn came, he bowed his head, paused nervously, and after struggling with his hands, proceeded to speak softly, and obviously from the heart. It was exciting just to watch him. He had come to the Unitarian Church not just to make conversation, to socialize, but because he was hungry to make contact. He felt lonely and isolated. Only sensation, the pain of contact, could bring him to life. But it was a difficult thing to ask women to do, especially in America.

"Last summer, however, while traveling in Sweden he met up with a woman, and without ever exchanging words they both knew that each was into what the other was into. For five whole days he had had all the painful contact he could wish for, and his only regret was that it ended as soon as it did.

"I had trouble understanding what he was talking about, and when I did I had even more trouble believing him. To me it was incredible that someone could be not only confessing but earnestly sharing with thirteen strangers that he was a sexual masochist who was intent upon continuing his obsession. For when the leader called "Time" and the group was about to break up, just in case he had not been explicit enough, Randolph quickly looked around and inquired, 'If any women here are interested, I'm available.'

"I don't know why that experience upset me so much. I'm a liberal. I realize that people have sexual hangups. Even though I'm not frigid, it takes an awful lot for me to relax sexually with a man, and after what happened with Charlie, I'm not sure I ever will again. So it's not that I'm naive or prudish, which is what a lot of men tell me, or that I originally found him so appealing. But it kind of deflated my idealism. It made me realize, I think, that if I stayed on in the singles scene, no matter how honest and straight I was, I would eventually wind up feeling contaminated."

Becoming romantically soiled was for Emily the worst of all fates, and to avoid it while continuing to search for the appropriate partner she began energetically to sample the available alternatives: Sunday brunches in cafés or tasteful restaurants, elegant buffet dinners with accompanying dance music, special singles parties promising to supply some of the more elite bachelors still left in New York City, and mammoth networking functions, supposedly combining business and pleasure, attended by throngs of circulating people, most of them eager to make contact and promote themselves in whatever way possible.

When she ran into the Revelers, an unassuming singles club occupying a second-story loft area in a building near Union Square, she stopped looking. Not because she was by any means satisfied, but simply because there was a conspicuous absence of things she did not like. There was not an overflow of flashy, clothes-conscious types. The two adjoining rooms were relatively small, dimly lighted, and comfortably furnished. People ranged in age between thirty-five and forty-five, and did not seem particularly sexually aggressive. While conversation certainly did not run deep, at least it was possible to sit down with someone and talk as long as one cared to: the music that was routinely turned on in the latter part of the evening was deliberately kept down in volume so as not to intrude upon people who did not want to hear it.

As for the dancing, she did not do disco, fast dancing, or the kind of dancing where two people, leaning on one another, merely swayed. On the rare occasion when she did accept an invitation to dance, it was to a sentimental, old-fashioned ballad, at a safe distance apart, with a man who struck her as comparatively wholesome. Honestly, she would rather watch than participate in the dancing, and she felt the same way about the endless circulating, milling about, and sporadic chattering that seemed to comprise much of the evening's ritualistic activities.

Because she gave off signals that she wanted to be approached only on her own terms, she was generally left alone, which was good. And she continued to use the line that she wanted to be "just friends," although she knew it regularly turned off men who might be interested in her. After many months on the singles scene, and innumerable disappointments, with the deadline of her forty-first birthday rapidly approaching, she was tired of nebulous hopes and wanted something solid and true or nothing. So she would continue to frequent the Revelers, in spite of her bad experience with the proprietor, Calvin McGrath, who had told her to go home, partly because she now felt supported by therapy, and partly because she believed she had exhausted her other options on the singles scene, and could now objectively say that she really did have nowhere else to go.

Then, serendipitously, or perhaps merely surrendering to unconscious pressures that were too much to bear, she met a man who she cautiously believed might be the one: a very nice guy, in touch with his feelings, who could communicate well, who did not talk trash or bullshit and have sex on the brain (he simply nodded when she indicated she wanted to be just friends). There were no drawbacks except one: he had been divorced six months previously, and if experience had taught her anything, it was that men on the rebound are scarcely reliable when it comes to availability. But that did not seem to be the case with Jeffrey, and even if it was, she was patient enough and strong-minded enough, especially if she had what she wanted in sight, to wait it out until he was available.

Emily had not been this excited since she had met Charlie, and that was quite ironic because they were scarcely similar. Where Charlie was extroverted and rough-hewn, like her father, Jeffrey was introverted, subdued, and deeply thoughtful. Where Charlie had pressured her constantly to have sex with him, Jeffrey, although he did seem puzzled as to the status of their dates (were they just friends or more?), scarcely brought the subject up.

On their first date Emily took Jeffrey on a tour of her favorite haunts in the Village, and encouraged by his lack of aggressiveness, surprised herself by volunteering to hold his hand, something she had never before initiated. On their second date, she was kissing him freely and warmly on the lips when it was time to say good-bye. And by the third, another first for her, she had invited him into the privacy and intimacy of her apartment, and begun to fantasize about if and when she might be ready to neck with him.

Much more important than the way Jeffrey appeared to honor her platonic needs was the manner in which he treated her. He not only listened to her, he paid attention, and whatever he said, whether she agreed with it or not, she almost always found perceptive and original. And believing that she alone had been responsible, had kindled such exquisite responsiveness, she gradually revealed herself as she had not done for years. She spoke wistfully and frankly of her decline from a once topflight, award-winning graphic arts designer into a part-time freelancer, someone who had to struggle to make ends meet and who often was unable to pay even her moderate rent without the help of her loyal father in the Bronx. She spoke of the central relationship of her youth, and of the reasons why she believed it had failed, and she even spoke, cautiously, of her recent obsession and infatuation with Charlie—omitting, of course, her peculiar night, the hands of the clock that had magically moved backward instead of forward, her subsequent confinement in Lenox Hill Hospital, and the Haldol which she continued to take. To her astonishment and delight, Jeffrey accepted everything.

When I asked Emily if she had considered whether such undoubted sensitivity and kindness might not be a basic feature of his personality and not just evoked by their relationship, she impatiently brushed the question aside. Jeffrey was responding to *her*, she was certain. During the six weeks that she had known him, he had proven many times that he was her special friend. Now, especially with her forty-first birthday nearing, there was no further need to wait.

And on their very next date, she surprised Jeffrey by suggesting that instead of their going out, he come to her apartment so she could cook him dinner. Of course he agreed, as she knew he would, but there was a tentativeness in his voice she could not ignore. So she made sure to make light of the lace dress she had worn for the occasion ("this is the full trap"), the three-course meal, the dimmed lighting, the music, before taking his hand in hers and nervously and painfully reciting how, now that she fully trusted him as a friend, which was the really important, the really difficult part for her, she was ready for more.

"More?" echoed Jeffrey in a peculiar flat voice.

Suddenly she felt as dazed as he appeared to be, but she was determined to go ahead with what she had rehearsed so many times in her head that she did not have to think about how to say it. Yes, more. She was fed up with the singles scene and wanted a real relationship. She did not doubt that she had the capacity to be fully intimate with a man and to make him happy, but she needed to know that she had found the right one. Gently she squeezed Jeffrey's hand and looked into his eyes. Although it was not necessary for Emily that the right man be handsome, Jeffrey had fine bone structure, an almost perfectly shaped head, distinguished silver-tinted hair, and remarkably sensitive brown eyes. Feeling much more emotional than she had anticipated, she heard herself murmur, "You're a very nice guy."

He apparently understood that for Emily it was a statement of great romantic import, and he responded by instinctively withdrawing his hand, becoming formal and frozen, as he typically did whenever he felt threatened or pressured. But he had little choice except to be direct.

"Emily, I thought you meant it when you said all you wanted was to be just friends. That's all I wanted too. I do like you very much and I've enjoyed our dates, especially the conversations we've had. It's not that I only want something platonic, but I'm definitely not ready for a serious relationship, and I realize for you there's no such thing as casual sex."

Sensing that concealed beneath Jeffrey's gentlemanly attempt to shoulder the blame for the alleged misunderstanding was an unvarnished rejection, Emily became desperate and enraged. She could not, would not accept that the hopes she had pinned on Jeffrey were as empty of promise as the ones she had nourished nearly a year ago for Charlie—and for about three hours, with both bitterness and logic, she tried to convince him that it was only fear of intimacy, as it had been with the others, and nothing else, that made him want to retreat. When it was finally over, when she was too exhausted to continue arguing and too hopeless to believe anything could ever come of it, she sighed, "I guess I'm trying to prove with logic that this is the right relationship for you, which I know is impossible."

Her realization left her spent, defeated, and wondering if she was perhaps too haggard-looking ever to get a man to love her. When she next saw me, she expressed the fear that perhaps such gloomy thoughts were the beginning of a second episode that would send her back to the hospital. She reminded me that she still believed the hands of the clock had somehow spookily turned backwards, but she added that it did not seem so significant to her now as it once had, and she seemed comforted that the night after Jeffrey had left, which had been sleepless and miserable, had not been at all *peculiar*. Even if I denied it, she told me, she was certain that my secret personal opinion of the singles scene was that it was rotten, maybe even bullshit, and that it probably held nothing of value for her.

So, she concluded brightly—as though simply relaying information concerning a key discovery and decision that she had independently arrived at—she was going to extricate herself from an excruciating no-win situation. Although she would go on, in her own way, searching for the ideal partner, having resolved never to give up, at least she would not continue to do so on the singles scene.

THE LOVE ADDICT

Although Emily would disagree, and certainly did not see her quest as an obsession or an abnormal craving, love for a variety of reasons can become one of the most addictive of all emotional states. First of all, if only for brief stretches of time, it can feel purely pleasurable, in the way that a drug can, and to that extent can appear to promise the brightest and best future (narcissistic giving). In its capacity to limit choices, lend a sense of purpose, convey a feeling of existential destiny ("this was meant to be"), it can overcome ambivalence and unify the sense of self. And just because such attributes are so often considered positive, they can be conducive, given the right antecedent conditions of deprivation and neediness, to feelings of dependency and attachment. Which is another way of saying that whatever is unique, attractive, and compelling about being in love can, under adverse psychological circumstances, make it the target of an addiction. And to appreciate how potent such an addiction can come to be, it may be helpful to examine some of the standard although extraordinary benefits love can confer—which are:

It is an emotional state that can be simultaneously an intense source of pleasure.

It is an urgent, sometimes crisis-prone state, in which striving for the attainment of the love object may eclipse everything else, and thereby intensely focus and totally absorb the lover.

It is a dramatic state, imbuing one's life with storybook suspense (will it end happily, with two lovers finding and staying with one another?). Analogous to the smokescreen effect of a nightmare, one of the things that enables a person to survive a nightmarish experience (e.g., Matthew in California) is the diverting presence of suspenseful elements. It is as though it is so important to mobilize defenses in order to survive that there is neither time nor leisure to dwell on such subordinate issues as how unhappy one is or how much one is suffering, as in Viktor Frankl's poignant observation (1959) that suicides are rare in concentration camps. It follows that being in love can serve to transform much of the anxiety concerning the day-to-day intimacy needs of routine interpersonal transactions into a suspenseful anxiety over the eventual outcome of the center-stage romance. For a time, such suspense may achieve the status of a leading narrative —not only a function and product of language (Roy Schafer, 1976), but a dynamically actualized and specified defense against an underlying, unstated, and more global anxiety.

It is a great filler of time, and to the degree that it is usually pregnant with suggestions for things to be done in order to obtain the object of one's desire, it can structure a life.

It can seem sensual and daringly hedonistic, inasmuch as the lover on one level appears to be genuinely pursuing something solely for the gratification of the self. Yet, since the love object is usually believed to be intimately and powerfully connected with one's sense of self, being in love can also feel as if one is working on achieving an integration or enrichment of the inner self at the core level. Viewed this way, being in love is like being in the throes of elemental passions: a rare and heightened state of pleasure, promising extended relief from the banalities of daily emotional life.

It can seem like suddenly becoming unrepressed, liberated, and surprisingly in touch with a dormant unconscious. Since people normally do not experience, or admit to experiencing, emotions as intense as romantic love (conventionally occurring only a few times, if at all, in the course of a lifetime), when it does happen, it can appear, in its magical excess, as though something profound has been released from the depths of the person and is involuntarily expressing itself. In the psyche of the lover, this sense of something having forcibly broken through can be equivalent to a heady loosening of the habitual repressive barriers to deep emotion.

Thus the overvaluation of the reciprocating lover can feel like a wondrous accomplishment, and the resulting expanded self-esteem can seem more meaningful and real, in its concentrated intensity, than the sum total of applause and reinforcement garnered in the past. Conversely, to lose such an overvaluation (which Freud explained as being caused by the beloved having captured the ego ideal), can be experienced as losing an indispensable anchor of fundamental self-respect.

It may be the most anthropomorphic of all states of mind, inasmuch as it can seemingly reduce the complexity of the universe to an interaction between two people. Freud described three heavy blows dealt to the narcissism of man in the course of history: the theory of Copernicus stating that the sun, and not the earth, was the center of the galaxy; Darwin's theory of evolution showing that human beings had evolved from primates; and the theory of psychoanalysis itself, depicting how man was not even the master in his own house (i.e., he was the servant of his own irrational unconscious). In his seminal work of 1914, Freud conceived of an original state in which the infant, who has not yet learned how to differentiate, conceptualize, or relate to an object, invests his primitive pleasure ego in aspects of himself. Freud called this stage a primary narcissism (self-love), and he considered it a normal stepping-stone to a higher, more developed love, object love (or love of another person). In spite of this, the longing for the exquisite joys and privileges of infantile primary narcissism is by no means completely relinquished, and in a variety of ways it continues to exert a dynamic impact upon subsequent behavior.

One of these is the consolidation in the psyche of the ego ideal, which exists, in no small measure according to Freud, in order to recapture and redirect the flow of the libido away from the outer world of sundry love objects and back to the narcissistic craving of the abandoned ego. Another, of course, is the dramatic conquest of the favor of the beloved (who by definition has already captured the lover's ego ideal), which invariably betokens a resuscitation and return to at least a portion of the original narcissism felt to have been lost. It is in its capacity seemingly to restore the lover to the position of autonomous hub of his own private narcissistic world that the condition of being in love can be so gratifying.

The psychoanalyst René Spitz (1965), in his classic studies on hospitalization, showed that the absence of human contact in the first months of life, even where all the primary biological and healthcare needs were being met, could in some cases lead to the infant's death, evidence of the vital importance of interpersonal relationships from the beginning. If the intensity of withdrawal pains is one measure of the strength of an addiction, and if the unnatural and imposed withdrawal from human contact (in the extraordinary cases of the foundlings deprived of minimal tactile stimulation who were studied by Spitz) can actually lead to death, this is at least suggestive of how potent in later life may be the addiction to another person that is sometimes characterized as obsessive love.

In fact, in some ways addiction to a love relationship is much more powerful than addiction to a drug, inasmuch as: with a drug there is one fundamental biochemical variable and a more or less predictable schedule of reinforcements (i.e., the average expectable effects following ingestion of the drug), but with a person there are always numerous variables to contend with, and it is therefore no accident that people who feel addicted to loving are often confused as to the reasons for the addiction—e.g., "I don't know what it is, or why it is that I love him (or her) so."

According to learning theory (Skinner, 1936, 1938), the addictiveness is intensified when the schedule of reinforcement is inconsistent and noncontingent. If we apply this to the obsessed lover, we can see that because he never knows for sure what kind of response he is likely to receive from the target of his obsession, his addiction is correspondingly less predictable, less manageable, and to that degree more compelling. And although Skinnerian behaviorists like to divide behavior into that with a contingent and that with a noncontingent schedule of reinforce-ment, and seem to believe that they can isolate behavioral vari-ables, establish a reliable data base, and (in the case of contin-gent reinforcement) confidently predict a response, which cer-tainly may hold true, provided that one and only one variable is extrapolated from the mosaic of dynamic human behavior, it may be even more revealing to compare, not one behavior with another, but behavior with nonhuman addictive chemicals and behavior with addictive human partners (lovers).

It follows that a psychoanalyst who is thinking along the lines of contingent reinforcement, instead of looking for isolated lin-ear stimulus-response sequences, will study the relationship as a whole, its reinforcement or deprivation in a variety of holistic sit-uations and from a hierarchy of response levels.

This difference between the quality of addictiveness to a drug and to a human being is reflected, as would be expected, in the respective withdrawal symptoms. For example, the "crashing" from the high of a drug such as cocaine, depressing as it may be, does not necessarily entail a loss of self-esteem. By contrast, when a love relationship is unexpectedly and involuntarily terminated, there is invariably a loss of self-esteem. Since withdrawal from a drug obviously does not involve feeling rejected by the drug, as with another person, it does not directly threaten the ego ideal (as a lover's indifference always does). A closer analogy, there-fore, between withdrawal from a drug and withdrawal from a love object would be in the case of actual bereavement: the crucial dif-ference being, of course, that the addict, unlike the widow or wid-ower, can instantly end his withdrawal symptoms, and his mourn-ing, the moment he chooses to reinstate use of the drug.

On the other hand, there is also an analogy between withdraw-ing from a drug and leaving a loved one. Both are rejections, and to that extent can represent being in control, but there is a differ-ence: the recovering addict, even if he has bottomed out, is always the one to reject the drug (it is no small part of the appeal of the addictive chemical substance that it can never reject the user).

Unlike a drug, which affects one person at a time, an obsessive love can seem an almost equally potent way to control the behavior of the other as well. This is because it is natural for the obsessed lover to project his own addiction onto the beloved and, through projective identification, subsequently believe that the object of his addiction is similarly addicted, i.e., like one junkie viewing another. And even if the other does not respond to the obsessional and provocative acting out in the hoped-for, reciprocally addictive way, enormous attention can nevertheless be coaxed or coerced by the pathology of love (as in the alcoholic enabler), which can easily be confused with a corresponding addiction.

Often the obsessed lover receives sympathy, even permission to continue to act out narcissistically and self-indulgently, which is attributable in part to what may be called the Blanche Dubois syndrome—that someone spurned or unlucky in love is perhaps the most wounded of all animals on earth, a veritable emotional cripple.

Consequently, a tormented lover is often conceived of as an honorable and therefore tragic beggar, and the equation is set up in the unconscious between obsessive loving and begging: the deserted lover being regarded as one who has been wrongfully deprived of something as indispensable to happy and healthy living as food, money, or shelter. The difference is that in order to deny that people can be so out of control of their lives that they can wind up legitimately destitute, the beggar is generally blamed and held responsible for his condition. By designating the beggar's state of public helplessness as a self-induced one, a way is found to create distance between oneself and the beggar's lot.

By contrast, the state of the discarded, wounded lover is considerably easier to identify with, since it is more acceptable that one has lost the love of the love object (over which there is no control). And because there is such a tendency to pardon the bereft lover, while disdainfully distancing oneself from the beggar, the similarity between the two is frequently overlooked—that both passionately believe that their tarnished self-esteem can only be restored from without.

Seen in this light, it is no accident that the reasons which the beggar employs to psych himself up to beg—that his condition is unfair, unnatural, and too much to bear—resemble the rationalizations jilted lovers use to implore their disinterested former partners for a second chance: that all they want is an opportunity to repair and replenish a piece of themselves that has been unkindly wooed away. Denying the plight of a homeless person or beggar is in part a refusal to grant that much control over the basic fate of the self to external contingencies: in other words, the denial consists of maintaining that it is entirely up to oneself whether one becomes a beggar or not.

In the case of unrequited and obsessive love, however, the perception can be reversed: people consider it an act of courage to risk everything by placing one's self-esteem in the hands of another and they are often willing (when this traumatically backfires, as in the case of unrequited love) to lay the blame on the lack of warmth, nurturance, and empathy of the other. To do the same with regard to the homeless person or the beggar is to acknowledge that it is possible not to have the resources even to survive physically with dignity. The emotional risk of obsessing over love—because love is considered so much higher than mere survival— is that much more acceptable when it fails. By contrast, the beggar who delegates the responsibility for his physical and existential self-maintenance to anonymous persons or agencies is looked down on as unwilling to take the risk of self-care on his own behalf.

Opposing this traditional contempt for begging is the current wave of support for New York City's multiplying numbers of homeless, and their sympathetic portrayal as largely victims of social injustice, which in part seems to be a denial of the extent to which their plight is a direct result of their internal failure to provide psychic self-care. And attributing their plight to the inequities of housing policy and the insensitivities of government is a way of romanticizing their predicament by making it analogous to the loss of a disinterested lover, something that is tragically out of their control.

To the degree that the rejected lover is seen as a tragic beggar, it is that much harder to say no, and therefore, that much more tempting to persevere in begging: i.e., the obsession is reinforced. Whereas with the anonymous beggar there is only survivor's guilt ("there but for the grace of God go I") to contend with, in the case of the imploring lover the accusation is incomparably stronger: instead of look what happened to me and look what they did to me, it's look what *you* did to me.

In spite of the fact that it is unquestionably harder to say no to a pleading lover than to an unknown mendicant on the street, it is also true it is even more difficult to say yes. For here yes means not nominal recompense, but the committment of a significant part of one's self, and that, of course, can be terrifying to someone who has already decided that it is impossible if not emotionally dangerous to resume intimacy with a former romantic partner now perceived as a deterrent to further growth.

For many people, the greatest impact they will ever have on another person, outside of their family, will be the impact on someone who falls in love with them, and the closest they are ever likely to come to being perceived as charismatic. And one of the most addictive qualities, therefore, of the state of being loved is the addiction to the novel feeling of being charismatic to at least one person: when someone is clearly acting as though under your spell; when the smallest details of your personality, magnified by the overvaluation of the lover, may seem of the highest interest. By contrast with the ordinary lover, the genuine charismatic personality wishes to have the whole group, not the individual, fall in love with him.

For the average person, however, the fantasy of being truly charismatic (i.e., loved by many) may be stimulated by encountering one person who responds to him romantically and who may represent perhaps the first nonfamilial individual who has truly perceived his objectively unique qualities, which had never before been appreciated. Being loved can therefore come to mean in the unconscious that the fantasy of one's infantile narcissism being redeemed and validated by someone from the outside real world has at last come true.

Because of this, regardless of how monogamous one is, the experience of being loved by a single person can seem to presage the advent of others who will similarly find cause for loving one, and will pay comparable (if appropriately more discreet and sublimated) homage. It follows that the perception of being loved may also be perceived as an omen of good fortune; now that it has happened once, it can happen again.

In his paper "Mourning and Melancholia" (1915), Freud pointed out that when the ego is sufficiently hated (as in melancholia), it perceives itself as dying, and gives up: and conversely, when the ego is gratuitously loved (as in mania), it perceives itself as exuberantly invincible. As Freud described them, and as they have generally been thought of since, melancholia and mania are two abnormal clinical states. But perhaps for the ordinary person, being loved, carrying with it the hope of being charismatic, powerfully triggers the fantasy of being loved by everyone. Inversely, rejection and abandonment by a lover can be equated with the hopelessness of ever recapturing the early state of blissful infantile narcissism by believing that one is at last being objectively loved.

From this standpoint, the charismatic personality is someone who has successfully nourished the hope that he can, on a consistent basis, be loved by many people, while for the rest of us, the road to charisma will be through romantic involvement with, usually, one person. This is another way of saying that for the average person falling in love can inspire the hope that the memory of being narcissistically admired by one's parents was not a family-romance illusion that must be surrendered, but may actually be reclaimed and vindicated, by a process of gradually being discovered and loved.

For all of these reasons, being in love is like entering an altered state such as being drunk or high, and it is immediately perceived by others as something quite different from ordinary behavior. Attention is quickly captured. People who were not interested in you before are apt to be interested in the unusual condition you have managed to get yourself into. There is probably no emotional state that inspires such vicarious interest—except, perhaps, a recent sexual experience—as being in love. The person in love, aware of such unprecedented envious curiosity in the details of his present emotional life, can begin to feel for the first time like a larger-than-life charismatic character on a stage. This is understandable, since love, in its capacity to involve the core of the self, can seem in itself a larger-than-life psychic state.

Because of this, people in love often feel entitled to act out more emotionally than they ordinarily do their hurt, anger, and jealousy, the unconscious justification perhaps being this equation: Since I feel more, I must express more. And it follows, when it comes to the jealous anger of an obsessed unrequited lover, that such justification can extend to acting out the wildest possible rage.

In this sense, being in love can also, especially when it does not end well, represent permission to regress and be primitive, which is yet another of its addictive qualities. In the case of jealous rage, the following toxic equation may come into play: Being deprived of the object of one's love is like being robbed of a vital part of the core of the self, and is as damaging as being physically robbed. Therefore, in certain instances it can justify even homicidal self-defense—for example, when surprising one's lover in the act of making love to someone else. In such cases, when the loss of love has been deemed traumatic enough to disrupt the fundamental balance of the psyche, by inciting violent retaliation, the legal system may allow the defense of temporary insanity. Which is to say, there is tacit juridical acknowledgement that under certain conditions a lover's jealous rage can be the psychic equivalent of the perception of a direct criminal assault.

THE LONELY HEART

At the center of the singles scene is the lonely heart and loneliness. Not the kind that the psychiatrist Harry Stack Sullivan (1953) wrote about, involving the difficulty (which he called a developmental warp) of even attempting to enter into an intimate relationship of any kind with another person, but the reverse. The loneliness of obsessive love is one of aftermath, of emptiness following the disillusionment that characteristically sets in. For obsessive love is not love, which by definition is founded on nurturing mutuality and true intimacy. Yet it is the very nature of it, to seem so much like love, that makes the inevitable realization that it is not so painful to accept. Which is also true of the despondent aftermath, or "crashing," so typical of drug abuse. Perhaps the mind is confused physiologically, and cannot tell the difference between endorphins released by the satisfaction of legitimate intimacy, the mood alterations of drugs, or the romantic longings of unfulfilled love. What is clear is that it is especially painful, just when you are certain that what you want is in your grasp, whether through drug-induced altered states or fantasized raptures of obsessive love, to be forced to deal with its inevitable disappearance.

Such pain can be misleading, for what can be more real than the suffering caused by heartbreaking rejection? And this may be why jilted lovers usually not only do not doubt that they are in love, but are never more sure that they are involved in the real thing than after they have been discarded (which may be due partly to denial that the pain they are going through is for anything less than true love—nothing less could justify their suffering).

Perhaps what is most lonely is the repetitiveness of obsessive love. By being unable to withdraw from the toxic side effects of non-intimate love, by impulsively becoming attached, disillusioned, or rejected, one exhaustively repeats the mourning process and does not allow it to be completed. Seen this way, the natural mourning process for the lost object, in the obsessive lover, is never finished because it is never allowed to begin: a consequence of the inability to accept that one can not possibly control the romantic feelings of the other.

Finally, the loneliness of the obsessed lover is caused not only by the absent love object but by the obsession itself. For underlying it, the addicted person knows, on some level, that there is a frightening lack of ability to provide for oneself what it is one most needs, and a correspondingly desperate restitutive attempt to make an outside agency or person responsible. It follows that no matter how good, or momentarily secure, such a person feels, there is the haunting fact that should he suddenly stop feeling good, there is no backup power within to continue to make himself feel good. This is another way of saying that without the comforting sense of a stable inner source of self-nourishment, the threat of abandonment cannot be far away.

By constantly reenacting the drama of pursuit, rejection, and loss, as Emily did, feelings of desertion will be reinforced and the expectation of loneliness will automatically increase. This may be no accident, obsessive love being perhaps an unconscious strategy for remaining lonely so as not to have to confront intimacy: and this is why it places the rejection by the other in the foreground and sees as its greatest goal to reverse and undo it (presumably so as to undo the pain). But paradoxically, the very fact that the primary relationship in obsessive love is the relationship one has to rejection—whether positively controlling it or negatively being unable to—can only contribute sooner or later to cumulative feelings of absence and deprivation, once again adding up to loneliness.

There is a sense in which it is more painful, in part because it is more lonely, to be a love addict than a drug addict. If he can find the money and the connection, the drug addict can always acquire the object of his obsession. The love addict, by the nature of rejection, cannot have the object of his desire. Therefore, he is like someone who is suffering almost continuously from withdrawal pains, which, unlike the drug addiction, do not have a natural and biochemical termination, and which is one more reinforcement of loneliness.

Not surprisingly, singles-scene gatherings scattered throughout urban centers in America, as in Manhattan, will seek to combat such disheartening loneliness. A favorite strategy is outright denial, and accordingly, those who frequent singles scenes almost invariably act like cheerful, pleasant, fun-loving people in control of their lives. Disco music frequently blares. Conversation is deliberately light-hearted, sending the message that nothing serious is at stake. The most positive thinking of philosophies are bandied about (EST, scientology, and so on), and the last thing anyone seems to want to admit is that he or she is lonely, hurt, confused, obsessed, or emotionally out of control.

Entrepreneurs of singles places are quick to capitalize on such loneliness. The implication is that instead of throngs of lonely, obsessed people, there are multitudes of attractive, self-fulfilled, healthy people yearning and ready for intimacy; and it is analogous to the drug pusher's attitude that what he is offering is not only acceptable, it is a treat, something considerably more enjoyable than the rewards of daily living. And accordingly, what the singles scene promotes, and proclaims itself to be, is not a collection of lonely hearts, but a plethora of available lovers, all capable of intimacy, all milling about just waiting to be introduced to one another, just waiting for someone to say the magic word "Hi!"

CONCLUSION

BEHAVIORAL PUPPETRY

The Puppeteers of the title is a metaphor. It does not matter whether the strings are believed to be pulling from the outside (as in the case of Tony Thunder), from the inside (as with Emily), or from both directions (as with Matthew and Paul). What counts is a preoccupation with issues of control, an anxious need to gain power over oneself and others, or a dread of failing to do so and of being irresistibly manipulated. This is not control in the adaptive sense of healthy defenses and autonomous self-regulating. Rather it is the compulsion to get the upper hand that often results in human behavior becoming so stilted that it is seen essentially as a technique or a strategy rather than a process. And it is a central thesis of this book that such maladaptive control— not only in relationship to oneself and others, in the bizarre indoctrination practices of cults, but also embodied in such mainstream professional roles as selling and advertising—is widespread in contemporary culture.

When behavior is thought of this way, as technique, a strategy, or the product of puppetry, it is often conceived of as a discrete unit: something that is indiscriminately pushed or pulled along, like cars in a train, by a unitary force. It is characteristic of such behavior that there is neither time nor inclination to contemplate multiple-level causation or overdetermination. It is characteristic of this frame of mind that it feels goaded by urgency and crisis, and views motivation as a kind of trigger: there is only one button to press, and it is a question of finding it. Behavioral puppetry resting on an unconscious perception that one is being controlled or dominated by a dammed-up excitation (analogous to a pres-

CONCLUSION

sure cooker) that must be released will often appear simplistic; and this is because psychological pressure, paralleling bodily pressure, does not allow the leisure or mental space in which to ponder alternative and more complex courses of action. For someone who feels, therefore, under the gun of a pressurized motivation, as the person preoccupied with issues of control almost always does, the most compelling impulse, overriding all others, will be to find the most expedient way to relieve the obsession.

In this light, an important reason for the addict's pursuit of the drug is not only in order to obtain short-term relief from unbearable tension, but because he has already been predisposed by addictive thinking to believe that satisfaction is to be found in only a simple, unitary agent. (As Freud (1915) showed, neurotic behavior is intrinsically restrictive, and one of the curative benefits of psychoanalytic psychotherapy was supposedly its ability to broaden options by undoing repressive restrictions.)

Behavioral puppetry can be divided, roughly, into feelings of dominating or being dominated (much more common). Feeling controlled from without is almost always preceded by projection; in other words, first there is an introject of primitive control, which is subsequently mapped onto another suitable person (much of the work that I did with Matthew, accordingly, focused on early family dynamics).

Although there will be the expected range of variations, when a person feels controlled, manipulated, seduced, or overpowered, whether from within or without, there are often some recognizable and consistent reactions. Such a person, as indicated, may regard his own behavior as relatively simple, comprised of a small range of motivations and entailing few options. There will invariably be hostility toward the self, especially whatever is perceived as controlling the self, resulting in a compulsive tendency to divide oneself up into parts that are controlled and parts that are autonomous. The philosophy that is compatible with this perception of the self is of life as a Darwinian power struggle: a good life is one that masters the tasks and musters the forces necessary to achieve satisfaction.

Someone who feels controlled by something or someone else feels abused. He harbors the paranoid suspicion that if he were more respected, he would be granted more space. Feeling controlled can become confused with being intruded upon. It is as though there were a telephone or doorbell ringing in the mind that won't stop. The implication is that one cannot fight off the intruder (and make it stop ringing), and is therefore weak. Or maybe the voice that is insistently calling knows something, and the message that is begging to be delivered is one that should be listened to. Maybe there is something that had better be done that is not being done.

Feeling controlled, therefore, feels like being pressured. Feeling pressured feels like being badgered. Feeling badgered feels like being punished. And feeling punished feels like being bad. It is easy to believe that if only one had more self-control, there would not be this need for an outside agency (or an accusing inner force) to take over.

And it is because such a person experiences the controlling influences as a kind of low-grade alarm, that is constantly going off, it is almost impossible to feel that it is safe to leave well enough alone and allow one's life to unfold spontaneously (and smell the roses). Nothing seems more obvious than that there must be activity and change, and that life is a matter of push and pull, of levers and manipulation, of cause and effect, of whether you wind up as puppet or puppeteer.

No one who feels continually harassed can avoid feelings of being deprived, unloved, and unfairly taken advantage of; they go with the territory. The suspicion grows that life is unfair, that there is little real mercy, and the lesson to be learned is that whenever there is power, it will be used. There is the cynical belief that relief from pressure will come only from meeting force with force, controlling what controls. It all leads to the demoralizing conviction that you will never be nurtured, that nothing will ever be given to the self when you are perceived as victim.

Feeling excessively controlled, therefore, breeds a survival psychology and automatically reinforces existing narcissistic tendencies. Behavior is perceived as effortful, since effort is needed to overcome whatever is holding one back, and accordingly cannot be easy or fluid. Instead, there is the pragmatic sense that what happens is the product of dynamic forces and conflicting strategies. And not surprisingly, it is difficult to feel creative when feeling controlled if only because the required space and freedom for creative play are painfully absent.

Still other characteristics accompany this state of mind. There will be a need to predict the outcome of events, so as to eliminate surprise. Since the only outcome that can be tolerated is relief from pressure, waiting can entail only unwelcome suspense and anxiety. There will be an irresistible tendency, therefore, to try to orchestrate the situation, to eliminate undesirable variables, and to oversee the process. It all adds up to what classically is called rigid behavior.

The underlying feeling of being controlled often results in defensively trying to produce behavior that may be perceived as a performance, a package or product. It is a corollary of this eventually to have the sense that one is somehow being objectified, behaviorally mechanized, emotionally pared down, and existentially reduced, so as to better be controlled.

Selling, seducing, living out a charismatic persona, attempting to indoctrinate someone into a rigid system of beliefs are all styles of human relating, in which the goal is to use a specific person as a means to an end. In which there is little interest in the interplay of mutuality and nurturance, as in intimacy. In which there is a predominant focus on control, and behavior is always calibrated by its outcome. (In retrospect, all of the behavioral pitfalls I have tried to illuminate in this book fall into the category of being directed toward a single predetermined outcome.) Once there is an emphasis on a unitary outcome, such as joining a cult, being seduced, reassuring an obsessive lover, or buying a product, that meets the need of only one person, there cannot be any hope of intimacy, which, in addition to mutuality and nurturance, is denoted by spontaneity, a trust in process, and a readiness to tolerate suspense about the future. Instead, there is a pressurized feeling of there being not enough time, of an impending deadline.

It is important to note that the inevitable power struggles that ensue can also be a defense, serving to alleviate anxiety over how to deal with neglected issues of intimacy. Perhaps because conflicts of power and control appear so clear-cut, urgent, concrete, and unambiguous, they offer the false comfort that something meaningful, which must be tended to, is about to be tackled. Ironically, even the addict believes, on some level, that he is accomplishing something when pursuing the object of his addiction. And in this light, being involved in power plays or control issues, whether as puppet or puppeteer, can convey a heady conviction that life has been radically reduced to bare essentials and is being lived out, and fought, on the basis of ultimate survival.

All of which effectively masks a covert deadness, and the natural, sometimes terrific, suspense (e.g., the storybook drama of obsessive love) as to who is going to win the power game further muffles the hidden, disavowed feeling of emptiness. Working strenuously to control oneself or others can hold out the enticing promise of being able to quantify behavior and thereby foster the illusion of having found a way to keep score (who's winning—who's losing).

And in the final analysis, it is the prospect of winning that may be the greatest allure of behavioral puppetry. For there are undeniably many short-term benefits from believing that control has been won and there is no doubt as to who is in charge. Now one can concentrate exclusively and comfortably on outcome, dispensing entirely with development and process, which means that a great deal less has to be contended with. Since the goal of interpersonal relationships is clearly nonreciprocal, this means sooner or later there will be an expectation of resistance—but this also means that one will be struggling only with defense mechanisms: experience of the other is therefore irrelevant, except as it impinges upon operational defenses. Part of the security of being in control is that one also has control over who does the rejecting, and does not have to worry about abandonment. To the extent that the person in command can orchestrate and dictate the tempo of a relationship, there is even partial control of time. And lastly, there is the belief that one is autonomous because empowered—yet another illusion, inasmuch as real freedom is freedom from the need to control.

One of the underlying assumptions of this book is that the psyche, like nature, abhors a vacuum, and if there is an absence of intimacy, then conversely there will be an excess of non-intimate behavior, in which preoccupation with control is a cardinal feature. What I call intimate behavior, at least in my experience— whether involving another person, one's own self, or one's work (which basically boils down to loving what you do)—is comparatively rare. There are many reasons for this, not the least of which is that ours appears to be a narcissistic culture with a matching focus on short-term and multiple gratifications.

The emphasis here, however, has been on the void that the lack of intimacy creates and the kinds of behavioral puppetry that fill it. In order to let the behavior speak for itself, I have tried to portray the patients as graphically, impressionistically, and phenomenologically as I could, reserving my comments and commentary for the end, and hoping to be unobtrusive as I attempt to make my interventions. Although these are surely not success stories, all the patients managed to use psychotherapy to free themselves from a meaningful portion of their obsessive behavior.

Matthew, who stayed the longest (five years), freed himself of his reliance on the charisma of another person. He not only developed healthy defenses against manipulative, intrusive people, but more important, learned to trust his own considerable resources and become increasingly available to feelings of intimacy.

Paul stayed two years, at which time he announced that he had accomplished his goal of finding a satisfactory non-harassing profession (he became an accountant). While he was able to see that the combination of his low self-esteem and fanatical denial led him into unfulfilling and painfully humiliating relationships with women, he was unwilling to let go of the behavior. And rather than surrender the extraordinary, although petulant, stubborn-ness, that seemed to be the cornerstone of his pride, he left therapy.

Emily, whom I regarded as clearly the most fragile of the three, stayed a year, long enough to muster the strength to abandon the singles scene. Although she refused to relinquish her quest for the ideal partner, we both agreed that her withdrawal from the singles scene was an important step.

As for Tony Thunder, he apparently never suffered a recurrence of the manic-depressive attack he experienced in California. Nor did he ever again endeavor to found or reestablish a cult. Instead, he returned to the motivational positive-thinking business, at which he had already proven himself by the time he was twenty-one, becoming increasingly successful (and even famous) in his late thirties—which says a lot, I think, about what it takes to succeed in today's business world.

The three people portrayed were chosen because they were particularly vivid examples of what it is like to be caught up in what I call behavioral puppetry. While their cases are admittedly extreme, it is my contention that what they broadly represent is widespread in our culture.

Excessively to control behavior—of oneself or another—promises the world and delivers almost nothing. Nevertheless, however, it has been and is being greedily oversold in this country. However appealing, compelling, or magnetic the idea of control may superficially appear to be, it seems to me that it is always worth resisting.

REFERENCES

Alper, G. (1992). Portrait of the Artist as a Young Patient. New York: Insight Books/Plenum Publishing.

Axelrod, R. and Hamilton, W. D. (1981). "The Evolution of Cooperation." Science 211: 1390–96. Reprinted in Evolution Now, edited by John Maynard Smith, 1982. San Francisco: W. H. Freeman and Company.

Berne, E. (1964). Games People Play. New York: Grove Press, Inc.

Bion, W. R. (1974). Experiences in Groups. New York: Basic Books, Inc.

Erikson, E. H. (1968). Identity: Youth and Crisis. New York: W. W. Norton & Company.

Frankl, V. E. (1959). Man's Search for Meaning. Boston: Beacon Press.

Freud, S. (1894). "The Neuro-Psychoses of Defense." Standard Edition 3: 58–61. London: Hogarth Press.

———. (1895). Studies on Hysteria. Standard Edition 2. London: Hogarth Press.

———. (1915). "Mourning and Melancholia." Standard Edition 14: 239. London: Hogarth Press.

———. (1915). "Repression." Standard Edition 14: 143. London: Hogarth Press.

———. (1922). "Group Psychology and the Analysis of the Ego." Standard Edition 18:65–143. London: Hogarth Press.

——— (1928). "The Future of an Illusion." Standard Edition 21:3; I.R.L., 15. London: Hogarth Press.

——— (1933). New Introductory Lectures on Psychoanalysis. Standard Edition 22: 120. London: Hogarth Press.

REFERENCES

Hauser, T. (1991). Muhammad Ali: His Life and Times. New York: Simon and Schuster.

Hill, N. (1963). Think and Grow Rich. New York: Ballantine Books.

Hoffer, E. (1951). The True Believer: Thoughts on the Nature of Mass Movements. New York: Harper and Row Publishers, Inc.

Laing, R. D. (1969). The Politics of the Family and Other Essays. New York: Pantheon Books.

Lifton, R. J. (1983). The Broken Connection: On Death and the Continuity of Life. New York: Basic Books.

Lorenz, K. (1970). Studies in Animal and Human Behavior. Vol. 1. Translated by Robert Martin. Cambridge, Massachusetts: Harvard University Press.

———. (1971). Studies in Animal and Human Behavior. Vol. 2. Translated by Robert Martin. Cambridge, Massachusetts: Harvard University Press.

———. (1981). The Foundations of Ethology. New York: Simon and Schuster.

Maynard Smith, J. (1972). "Game Theory and the Evolution of Fighting." In J. Maynard Smith, Evolution. Edinburgh: Edinburgh University Press.

Neumann, J. von and Morgenstern, O. (1944). Theory of Games and Economic Behavior. Princeton: Princeton University Press.

Ortega y Gasset, J. (1930). The Revolt of the Masses. New York: W. W. Norton & Co. Inc.

Schafer, R. (1976). A New Language for Psychoanalysis. New Haven: Yale University Press.

Shapiro, D. (1965). Neurotic Styles. New York: Basic Books.

Skinner, B. F. (1936). "Conditioning and Extinction and Their Relation to Drive." J. Gen. Psychol. 14: 296–317.

———. (1938). The Behavior of Organisms. New York: Appleton-Century-Crofts.

Spitz, R. A. (1965). The First Year of Life. New York: International Universities Press, Inc.

Sullivan, H. S. (1953). The Interpersonal Theory of Psychiatry. New York: W. W. Norton & Company.

Tinbergen, N. (1951). The Study of Instinct. London: Oxford University Press.

		DATE DUE	